Uncovering Mystery
in Everyday Life

Uncovering Mystery in Everyday Life

Confessions of a Buddhist Psychotherapist

R. J. Chisholm

Published in this first edition in 2022 by:

Triarchy Press

Axminster, England

info@triarchypress.net

www.triarchypress.net

A catalogue record for this book is available from the British Library.

Paperback ISBN: 978-1-913743-48-2

ePub ISBN: 978-1-913743-49-9

pdf ISBN: 978-1-913743-50-5

Cover illustration: 'Two Blind Men Crossing a Log Bridge' by Hakuin Ekaku.
Cover design: Bo Gort.

To Maya and Ricky, who will surely uncover mysteries of their own.

Contents

Introduction

This is a book about psychotherapy, and, though it addresses a theme that will be familiar to many readers, it does so from a somewhat unusual perspective. Psychotherapy is pretty much what it always has been: an ongoing relationship between two people – a psychotherapist and a client – which addresses the psychological difficulties and frustrations that afflict the life of the latter. Sigmund Freud originated the first form of psychotherapy with psychoanalysis, and it remains a prototype for virtually every approach today. But things have changed a great deal since Freud's day and few, if any, therapists would regard psychotherapy as the strict scientific, medical endeavour that he made it out to be. Although therapists may be well advised to draw from as much relevant scientific and medical knowledge as they can in dealing with their clients, the truth is that much of what happens in psychotherapy lies embedded in an unfathomable mystery. That is what this book is about.

But psychotherapy isn't supposed to be mysterious. It's supposed to be a rational way of treating various forms of mental distress as problems for which there should be attainable solutions. No client complaining of depression and anxiety, for example, would undergo therapy in order to be told that her condition is all a mystery. She wants relief and enters therapy with the hope and expectation that her therapist will have enough understanding and insight into her condition to help her find it. In fact, good, effective therapy will help her find ways to deal with her psychological misery to bring about improvement. But not all of the factors involved in her discovery may be entirely clear either to her or to her therapist.

Indeed, at the beginning of therapy, it may not be clear what the nature of the client's problem actually is, except, perhaps, for a vague, generalised feeling that her life is deeply unsatisfactory. Yet, this is when psychotherapy is supposed to assert its authority as a diagnostic discipline. But reaching insight may have less to do with understanding her condition diagnostically than it does with appreciating her experience existentially – that is to say, in all its inherent mystery.

The mystery that psychotherapy deals with may not always seem very mysterious. Therapy usually addresses everyday matters, the griefs and disappointments that are all too familiar to us all: the sense of betrayal that arises after a marriage or relationship fails; the sadness that refuses to fade long after someone close has died; the feeling of failure that appears to be preordained by fate. These are only a few of the common complaints that therapy deals with. But whereas the everyday world generally offers little more than well intended advice and sympathy, psychotherapy attempts to draw on an extensive body of knowledge to help people come to terms with their problems. Even so, a therapist is not some sort of mastermind of psychology who offers ready-made solutions to problems of the self. He (or she) is someone who tries to bring an informed perspective to what a client is experiencing, knowing that he can succeed only by helping the client reach decisive realisations for herself. Of necessity, then, therapy is a subjective, or rather, an intersubjective, attempt to make meaningful sense of the client's experience. One reason for calling it mysterious is that both parties are apt to be surprised by what their joint exploration will discover. But the mystery often goes further than that.

The idea that uncovering mystery could be a way of freeing someone from her psychological misery may seem almost magical, like consulting a ouija board or gazing into tea leaves in search of answers from the beyond. Even more dubious is the idea that a psychotherapist should act as some sort of wizard, or shaman of the unconscious who fathoms its mysteries with a tangential interest in the actual details of the client's life. Sometimes, a perceptive therapist actually can demonstrate an intuitive capacity that appears rather uncanny. But it is in the details and happenstance of the client's everyday world that the actual mystery of her life will most often be found. For the strong unconscious element in all experience plays out in the factualities that make up a person's life, and typically revolves around ordinary concerns such as family, relationships and money, though loss, grief and death also feature as common concerns of therapy. Familiar as these matters are from a disinterested point of view, when felt in the skin of actual personal experience they may still come as a surprise, sometimes even a shock, that can destabilise a person's sense of self. From a first person, subjective point of view – from the I-me-mine sense of self that forms the pivot of experience – intense psychological suffering will always have the power to catch anyone by surprise. The surprise itself points to a deeper, underlying mystery – the mystery of being existent at all.

Psychotherapy tends to take a dim view of such ultimate questions for good reason: contemplating things for which there can be no final answers may be a way of not facing up to matters for which answers *are* possible, yet difficult to find. Wondering about the existence of God, or the nature of reality, for example, may be convenient ways of avoiding a more immediate and addressable concern, such as the client's inability to form a lasting intimate relationship. Yet, imponderable questions about the fact and meaning of existence loom over everything we do. Such questions as "Why was I born?" and "What will happen to me when I die?" must – unanswerable as they are – remain in the background of the activities that comprise our everyday world. But a question that is closely related to those about birth and death rides on the pulse of experience: "Why am I as I am?". Psychotherapy should have no immediate answers to offer, and a therapist is usually wise in discouraging the client from idle metaphysical speculation. Yet, at the same time, questions about the self in the everyday world will often draw from the same source of wonder as questions about the unknowable reality beyond birth and death. Considered not as remote metaphysical speculations, but as logical extensions of ubiquitous questions of the everyday world – "where did I come from?" and "where am I going?" – the mysteries of birth and death converge on everything we do. This convergence has the power to provoke fundamental questions, though it is by living with such questions, rather than trying to answer them conclusively, that they become sources of meaningful wonder. Considered in the abstract, this may all seem rather remote. But it is part of the purpose of this book to show how immediate and compelling such questions can be.

The structure of the book will be familiar to anyone who has read other collections of psychotherapeutic tales. Similar to case histories, though less formal, therapeutic tales are brief stories about how therapists and their clients interact with each other in the course of therapy. Typically written from the therapist's point of view, these stories inevitably reflect the interests and values of the therapist as he recounts his dealings with his clients. For this reason, every collection of therapeutic tales should be unique, and the best of them do convey the inherent fascination of therapy. But there is a difficulty to achieving such originality, which affects psychotherapy itself, as well as the books written about it. Almost everybody believes they know what goes on in therapy, even if comparatively few people have direct experience of it themselves. Movies, talk shows, and comedy routines all make knowing references to therapy, and the kinds of problems that make people turn to therapy for help. So when someone mentions going to therapy for depression, for instance, we tend to dismiss it as a matter of everyday experience. Depression is in fact so common that, even if we don't suffer it ourselves, we all know somebody who is, or has been, depressed enough to seek treatment. But knowing something about any psychological condition, especially from hearsay or second-hand report, is hardly the same thing as understanding it from a psychotherapeutic perspective. In fact, even someone suffering from depression often has to free herself from the common sense understanding of her condition before she can reach any true insight into it. Psychotherapy often begins to find traction by helping her find a way of seeing beyond what she believes other people know to find a perspective that is uniquely her own. The hope of this book is that the stories presented here will help the reader appreciate what such an effort entails.

It may be obvious from what I have said so far that this book will be far more anecdotal (or, as I would prefer to express it, experiential) than theoretical, but it won't shun theoretical reflections when I believe they can offer insight. Though the book is not much concerned with theory, I do devote one chapter to the influence of Buddhist psychology on my practice as a therapist. I discuss this only to account for an important influence in my approach, not to proselytise for Buddhism as a religion. My idea is to present both the benefits and difficulties of using Buddhist psychological concepts for psychotherapy, though I know my peculiar brand of therapeutic syncretism may draw criticism from both psychotherapists and Buddhists alike. The criticism I fear most is that by trying to reconcile the concerns of Buddhism and psychotherapy, I am doing a disservice to both. I even concede there might be some truth to this criticism. But the value of any theory for me is the opportunity for critical reflection that it affords, and Buddhist psychology has always given me a wealth of things to reflect upon, both as a therapist and a practising Buddhist. Even so, every theory (to say nothing of every therapist) has its limits, and in my experience, psychotherapy always involves many more factors that any theory can account for. Fortunately, therapy isn't really about theory; it's about helping the client make sense of her personal experience in her everyday world. And though a therapist will often benefit by drawing on the insights that any good theory has to offer, when healing insight comes, it usually follows from the spontaneity and unpredictability of the therapeutic process, of one person sharing the mystery of her being with another person, in her search for meaning.

A final word must be said about the identity of the clients who feature in these therapeutic tales. When people come to therapy they don't want their inner lives to become a topic of general conversation. Moreover, protecting the confidentiality of clients is central to the ethics of psychotherapy, as privacy is essential for therapy as a relationship of trust. For these reasons, I have gone to some lengths to change many significant facts about the clients I discuss here, so much so that my presentations may be regarded as more fictional than factual. I have done this not only out of respect for the privacy of my clients, but also to give myself the freedom to speculate on matters that would be forbidden by confining myself to strict factual reports. Thus, in addition to changing names and a number of important biographical details, I have taken the liberty of making up some events, as well. The question may then be asked: if the names and identities, as well as significant events in the lives of the people I discuss have been so completely changed, how can these stories be said to be true at all? My answer is that while I have been careful not to be factual, I have tried to be as truthful as I could be in describing the nature of the work I do. With this caveat in place, I leave it to the reader to decide if I have succeeded.

Encounter

She arrives punctually for her first appointment and greets me in the reception room with clipped courtesy. Unlike many new clients, she betrays little interest or curiosity in me as she follows me into my consulting room. I gesture to one of two armchairs and invite her to take a seat, which she does with a faintly agitated air. I wait a moment as she settles in by shifting in her seat and turning off her mobile phone before putting it away in her handbag. I smile encouragingly but receive only a strained smile in return.

"Well, I'm Bob and you're ...", I begin, trying to break the ice.

"Kate", she interrupts before I can say her name myself.

"Yes, Kate. Okay."

"It's what everybody, all my friends call me. You can call me that, too."

"Sure – Kate. So, welcome. Maybe we can begin by you telling me what brings you here."

She fidgets and shifts in her seat as she seems to consider the question anxiously. Tension builds as the pause between my question and her answer lengthens. Perhaps she is worried about saying something wrong, or perhaps I have made some mistake in either my phrasing or vocal tone. Either way, the question carries more weight for her than I had intended. But at last she lets out a small determined sigh, and she begins to reply.

"Well, I am afraid", she begins but then stops immediately. I think she might be reaching for a phrase that will express her feelings precisely, but nothing comes out. Indeed, it seems more likely that something is refusing to come out.

"You're afraid of..." I gently prompt her.

"I am afraid... I am afraid I can't think of anything to say", she says with embarrassment. And then she retreats back into silence, leaving us both in suspense.

I think I know what is inhibiting Kate from speaking. She is anxious about coming to therapy and has doubts about what it can do for her. But far from not being able to think of anything to say, it is more likely that she has too many things to say and has been rehearsing a speech endlessly before coming to see me. But what she has to say if only she could lose her inhibitions will remain closed to me until she actually speaks. So I must wait without seeming impatient. I offer her a gentle smile.

The silence that occurs in therapy is seldom neutral or empty. It usually seethes with the unspoken content of the client's concerns and carries undercurrents of the therapist's feelings, as well. But unlike the client, the therapist should restrain his feelings rather than express them freely. I have to resist an impulse to reassure her, either by extolling the benefits of expressing herself openly, or by telling her that everything is going to be okay. Yet I don't want to hang her out to dry, either. Finally, I decide to say something.

"A lot of people feel tongue tied, especially when they first come in. Have you ever seen a counsellor or therapist before?" I ask.

She shakes her head, no, and I can see that she is still not ready to speak. There is nothing I can do at this point except to convey my willingness to listen with a readiness that is uninfluenced by impatience or expectation. Perhaps she will see it in my eyes, or in the way I sit back in my chair. My unspoken message to her is simple, so I hope that it is clear: speak to me and I will try to understand.

The idea that mere listening can provide help to someone may seem rather doubtful. Yet everyone would recognise that not being listened to, particularly in a moment of emotional need, would mean being cut off and ignored in the loneliness of one's self experience. Common courtesy requires that we should allow others their say and at least present the appearance of taking an interest in what is being said. But appearing to listen by feigning interest is not true listening at all, and can't begin to match the deep attentiveness that therapy requires.

What exactly is the therapist listening for? Signs or symptoms, clues that reveal some underlying pathology which drives the stress that makes someone seek therapy? Many people seem to think that therapy must begin with a diagnosis, an objective appraisal of the character – particularly the character flaws – of the client. But for me the beginning of therapy is less about identifying someone as a particular character type than it is about establishing a foundation for trust and deeper communication. Moreover, getting a clear idea about the client and her world is not a simple process that follows from a tick-box procedure of identifying character traits. It requires time and patience in order to allow deeper understanding to develop. It is led by a simple, if unspoken request: tell me who you are.

Eventually, Kate does begin to speak, which seems to open a flood gate of self-disclosure. The intense self-consciousness that she had been feeling has now given way to a free-flowing monologue and we both begin to feel relief. I can tell that she regards me as a sympathetic listener by the way she responds to my reactions, which are mostly facial, to her voluble speech. She tells me about her present unhappy relationship with a man she has never felt entirely sure of. She also feels that being in this relationship has something to do with her parents and the relationship they had when she was growing up. We both seem to be aware that this is a story that she has told before, certainly to herself, but also perhaps to her friends and other people she knows well. And though I don't doubt her honesty or sincerity at all, I do have questions about the predictable way her story unfolds. She appears to be working a formula, explaining her relationship in terms that might be found in books or magazines or television or in conversation with others. It is, she seems to believe, the way she is supposed to talk about her intimate concerns, and she seems to find comfort in having a ready-made way of talking about her emotional life. I follow her story attentively, though I refrain from making comments. I know that if she continues in therapy with me, I will have to encourage her to question the convenient self-narrative she appears to rely on. So what makes her turn to psychotherapy now, I wonder.

Psychotherapy is not everyone's preferred way of dealing with emotional pain. If family or friends are unable to provide support, people often turn to medications such as antidepressants to deal with their problems. Medication can be useful and in some severe cases, such as acute depression, it can actually be life-saving. But I am not sure how Kate believes her problem should be approached. She is anxious and depressed, and in spite of being able to voice her dissatisfaction, she believes her feelings run much deeper than the emotional frustrations that might have caused them. So she often wonders if there could be something biological, a chemical imbalance in her brain perhaps, that makes her feel at odds with herself. I explain that I am not a psychiatrist or neurologist, and I couldn't begin to make a medical diagnosis. Although I know some people do need medication to treat their mental conditions, I say, I also know that people often underestimate the power of their unexpressed emotions in the creation of their moods. I go on to say that moods are complex and involve both mind and body. We should not, therefore, rule out the option of seeking medication. But tell me, I ask, have you ever considered going to your GP for medication? Yes, she replies. She has often taken prescribed medication in the past.

Kate has been on and off antidepressants for years and has resorted to them whenever she feels the need by getting her GP to prescribe them for her. This is somewhat alarming, though quite familiar to me. Most GPs have only cursory training in psychological distress and are usually too burdened with an enormous caseload to listen to a patient mull over her feelings, especially when prescribing some pills and sending her along her way usually does the trick. The trick in question is to get the patient to leave the surgery without further complaint. Yet I can't assume that antidepressants are bad for her or that she would be better off pursuing psychotherapy without medication at all. So I ask her if antidepressants have worked for her in the past and if they have, why she came off them. She explains that although medication gives her relief from anxiety, they also make her feel slightly numb and out of touch with herself. I say nothing about this and withhold my ideas about the wisdom of her decision. In my view, whatever their benefits, antidepressants are greatly over-prescribed and are often given to people who might be better off without them.

I realise that part of her problem may be the desultory way she takes her medication without having her reactions closely monitored.

According to most psychiatrists, any psychoactive medication should be regularly checked and adjusted for changes in the patient's condition. Besides, even if she really does need medication, it would still be possible for her to be in psychotherapy. I do not, then, want to express any opposition to medication, especially now, before I get to know her well enough to form an opinion. But Kate hasn't come to me for my ideas about psychopharmacology. In spite of her suspicion that her problem could be biological, she also feels that there might be a hidden emotional reason for her distress and she hopes that I will be able to help her find it. She believes that her problem may lie in some hidden fount of anxiety that she can feel, yet can't quite locate, and she wants to know what the source of her anxiety could be. At this early juncture I know it would be unwise for me to speculate.

Many people think that psychotherapists must possess some special wisdom about the emotional lives of the people they deal with. As if the therapist, equipped with training in some theory of personality, should be able to peer freely into the client's inner world and find truths about her character that are hidden from her. The idea is seductive, but it can be dangerously mistaken, both for the client and the therapist. Although there are therapists who are informed, perceptive, sympathetic and perhaps even wise, whatever wisdom a therapist possesses must always remain in critical tension with what he doesn't know.

Moreover, therapeutic wisdom can never be distilled into an elixir of all-purpose insight. Insight has to be achieved through each relationship that the therapist develops with each new client. If there is a magic ingredient in this, it is trust. Gaining it takes time, as well as a certain elusive intuitive understanding that can only be developed with patience. This is something rather different from the belief that many clients hold about the therapist's expertise, which is supposed to enable him to provide definite solutions for ambiguous and conflicted life situations. So when Kate asks me if it is normal for her to have a partner who shows no interest in her feelings, I want to reply that her question is misconceived. Instead, I turn the question back on her.

"Well, that depends. Does it feel normal to you?"

"I don't know", she replies. "He acts like it's normal. And he's as normal as can be."

"Normal to him, perhaps", I observe. "But what about you?"

"I don't know", she repeats. But this time her reply conveys much more exasperation.

In fact, using the word normal to describe Kate's situation will provide little insight about her actual experience. Certainly her situation is nothing out of the ordinary, as she herself seems to realise. For unfulfilling relationships not only form a substantial bulk of therapeutic casework, they are, and always have been, the stuff of everyday conversation, too. Yet in spite of being so commonplace, being in an intimate relationship with someone who doesn't seem truly interested in you never *feels* normal. It feels lonely, isolating, and in the extreme, profoundly self-alienating. Still, given how often it happens, many people believe that being lonely in a relationship isn't abnormal at all. What catches Kate by surprise is how abnormal this supposedly common state of affairs makes her feel. It's a feeling of self-negation which makes her feel strangely disconnected from her usual sense of self. The feeling is actually more common than she realises and is one of the reasons for the booming trade in antidepressants. But the question that psychotherapy has always been concerned with is not only about how to help the client deal with the painful, apparently inescapable emotions that arise from difficult life situations. It is also learning about how a person came to be this way. This is an essential precondition for finding a better way of being.

I am aware that there are less than twenty minutes left in our hour together, and after our slow start, we seem to have made a good beginning. But there is much more to discuss than our remaining time will allow. Kate herself has made an intriguing observation that should not be overlooked, especially in light of her complaints about her present relationship. "You mentioned your parents earlier", I say. "What makes you think that they have anything to do with what you're experiencing in your relationship now?"

"Because", she replies, "I feel like I am turning into my mother."

"What makes you think that?", I ask, barely able to contain my interest.

"Well, I don't, really", she corrects herself immediately. And then she proceeds to list all the reasons why she is not, and could not, be like her mother. Unlike her mother, she is educated and tries to be independent and feminist in her outlook. Moreover, she has never identified with her mother who had always presented her with an example of what she didn't want to be.

"You must think that sounds awful", she says apologetically.

"I wouldn't say that. It's just the way you feel", I say reassuringly. "But how did you get along with your mum when you were growing up?"

"Not very well", she admits.

"And what about your dad?"

She begins to shake her head slowly before she actually begins to speak. "I hated him", she says quietly. "I still do."

"That sounds rather serious", I say softly. "Do you want to tell me why you feel that way towards him?"

"Because he's horrible and doesn't care about anybody but himself", she says with what sounds like understated defiance.

"I see", I murmur, though in fact I understand nothing except the strength of her aversive feeling for her father.

There is no denying that what Kate has just told me about her parents presents rich material for interpretation. Ever since Freud, most psychotherapy has operated on the axiom that what happens to someone in childhood carries over into adulthood without the full effect of those childhood experiences reaching conscious awareness. This can be seen in Kate's story. She knows that her relationship with her parents has influenced her deeply, yet she remains puzzled as to why it continues to haunt her. She is not, she insists, like her mother at all, nor does it seem likely to her that she would consent to be in a relationship with someone like her father. Yet, a feeling has increasingly taken hold of her that what she now experiences in her relationship with her partner is almost identical to what her mother must have felt in her marriage.

There are countless theories which confidently purport to explain why someone like Kate has so little insight into her predicament. Psychoanalysis, for example, would almost certainly find repression at work, while other theories might lay blame on the interpersonal dynamics of her family, or on a malign cultural influence such as patriarchy. And though theories that survive the passing of fashions usually do have some useful insights to offer, they can't all be appropriate for each specific case. Moreover, it is not what any theory says in advance of therapy that will illuminate a client's experience for the therapist. Its value is proven only in the course of therapy, in the shared experience of client and therapist. But this takes time, far more than the few minutes that we have remaining.

"We have only a few minutes left", I say, trying not to sound too abrupt. "Let me just say a few things about how this works." I then launch into a spiel about fees, appointments and cancellations, making it seem as if these practicalities are merely ancillary to the therapeutic process. In fact, clients often baulk at what therapy will require of them, both in terms of time and money. A common question that many clients ask is how long it will take to get better, as if there could be a timetable for treatment with a guaranteed positive outcome. But Kate simply nods as I speak which seems to indicate that she wants to proceed without any unreasonable assurances.

"I do think therapy may be able to help you make sense of things", I say in conclusion. "And if you think I can help, I would be happy to work with you."

She nods again, but says nothing. It seems as if she might have reverted back to being the buttoned-up presence she was when she first came in. Then she speaks.

"Should I set an appointment with you now or at reception?" she asks.
"At reception. I'll go with you to see what the availability is", I reply.

*****

After I leave Kate in the reception room I go back to my consulting room to record some notes which consist mostly of my impressions, as well as a few essential facts. She was my last client of the day so I have ample time to reflect on our first session.

First impressions in therapy can be as mistaken as anywhere else, but they will still have an effect that will carry over into our next session. These impressions go beyond the information she has given me, and include such non-verbal recollections as her facial expressions, posture and tone of voice. All of these impressions have already begun to coalesce in memory as a sense of her presence which will gradually deepen as I get to know her better. I know, too, that she will have a sense of my presence drawn from our first encounter. But of necessity, she has been far more self-revealing than I will ever be. Although therapy should, as R. D. Laing once expressed it, "be an obstinate attempt by two persons to recover the wholeness of being human in the relationship between them", the primary concern of our encounters will always be her experience, not mine. Fortunately, I am fairly certain she knew that I was listening to her sympathetically and not subjecting her to an examination with a cold, critical eye. This will, I hope, provide us with a good foundation for working together with increasing trust. But I won't be able to tell if our nascent alliance will hold until after we have met for at least several sessions.

I look over at the empty chair where all of my clients sit, and I think of the emotional tone of our encounter which still seems to linger in the consulting room. People who try, and then quit therapy shortly thereafter, often complain that what most discourages them is the emotional distance that their therapists exhibited. They felt judged and condemned, even though their therapist may have said nothing at all critical. Still, though therapists should be more inclined to listen than speak, listening can be carried out in a variety of emotional registers. The danger is that in the confessional setting of therapy a therapist may fall unwittingly into the role of a stern, forbidding judge. The cool neutrality he exhibits may seem to foretell a withholding of sympathy that many, if not most clients, crave. Although he may be trying to use silence artfully in order to elicit a thoughtful response, this can hardly be a straightforward undertaking. Listening will always be conditioned by both the intentions and presentation of the therapist, if not in quite the way that therapists hope, or their clients fear. Some therapists may say little because they want to offer a blank slate for the client to fill in. Others, I suspect, say little because they don't know what to say. The important consideration is whether the silence of the therapist feels safe and welcoming to the client, or is experienced as a tense boundary that will never be crossed. The question is not easily answered, but the answer will always be an important factor in whether or not the therapeutic relationship can succeed. Fortunately, at least in this first session, I believe that Kate had enough confidence to offer me a window into her world. If I am to succeed as her therapist, it is a world I will get to know very well.

Talking about a client and her world is simply a shorthand expression for the relationships and arrangements that make up her life. It can refer to relationships with parents or children, spouses or lovers, rivals and enemies, as well as the physical and social spaces that she inhabits. It is less a terrain of stable interests than it is an open sphere of shifting involvements playing out in time. Plans unfold and unpredictable events occur within it, but it all revolves around a sense of self that can only be known as '*me*'. Though it is often a frustrated, sometimes even fractured, sense of self that takes someone into therapy, there is no way of knowing what someone's sense of self is without learning about her world experience, too. But learning how someone experiences herself in the world will always be restricted by what doesn't come to light in the therapeutic encounter. Although the client may not be concealing, or consciously dissimulating about her experience, some important features of it may still not be communicated to me, especially in the early stages of therapy. Perhaps, as psychoanalysis says, she may be blocking something from her awareness by repressing it. Then again, perhaps I am missing something because I am not perceptive enough to notice it. But it may also be that we are both blind to things that influence our encounter without either of us being aware of these factors. For I inhabit my world, just as Kate inhabits hers, and some of the things that drive her intentional actions cannot, especially at this beginning stage of therapy, be evident to me. As we become better acquainted, my hope is that we will find a shared perspective from which we can see beyond our initial limitations, and discover what she actually experiences in the world she inhabits.

But for now, everything lies shrouded in a certain mystery.

I seldom talk about the mystery of psychotherapy with my clients, and I have no intention of telling Kate that there is something inherently mysterious about the process we are going to embark on together. Yet, the sense of mystery that I feel with each client is essential to the way I work. This doesn't involve anything like an occult initiation, nor is it about unearthing some dark, traumatic secrets, though such dark revelations can often emerge in therapy.

The mystery is more about recognising the unknown dimension of her experience and pulling away a veil of false knowledge and automatic assumption, perhaps to discover how much her sense of self is constructed out of hearsay and thoughtless conjecture. Helping a client realise that her self-understanding can be improved by examining her mental habits is essential for her to become more self-aware. But unearthing those deeply buried habits and exposing them for examination takes patience and time. Dealing with them abruptly could be deeply unsettling, perhaps even traumatising for her. Yet, if therapy succeeds in developing a relationship of trust, it will enable her to look deeply within herself to face uncertainties and find possibilities that she hadn't seen before.

I think back again to Kate's unwanted identification with her mother, and the sense of thwarted possibilities which that identification seems to cause her. Although she seems willing to look at her parental relationships, I can't be sure what she will permit herself to see. I also think about her relationship with her father and wonder what experiences might have caused the bitterness she expressed for him. But I am getting ahead of myself, and I am in danger of making unwarranted assumptions about her family relationships. Still, I have to remain alert to my hunches and intuitions, even though my ideas may later prove mistaken. Whenever I begin to work with a client, I often feel a need to strike a balance between intuition and doubt. It often seems that reaching an accurate understanding of a client requires me to entertain a number of incompatible ideas before I settle on one as more or less true. Perhaps this is what Freud meant when he advised analysts to listen to their patents with evenly suspended attention. Whatever it might be called, it hardly seems scientific.

Many people believe that psychotherapy is a profession similar to medicine and that psychotherapists have an expertise in diagnosing mental illnesses, which allows us to cut through our clients' discourse with a sharp clinical eye. But it's not really what I believe, or how I work. To me, Kate doesn't seem mentally ill, nor do I believe she suffers from a personality disorder. At this early juncture, she just appears anxious and prone to depression, though these are only first impressions. But if my questions are informed, attentive and, perhaps above all, caring, I may get to know her well enough to see what I can't see now.

Like many therapists, I often question my skills and wonder what would make me a better therapist. These doubts come up routinely in supervision, but the concern is most alive in dealing with a new client. How should I speak to Kate? No less important, will I know when to remain quiet? Freud called psychotherapy the talking cure, but it could just as well be described as a listening cure, though the manner of listening is all important. Attentive, sympathetic listening, I believe, offers the client a space for self-questioning that can often be more revealing than a pointed interrogation, precisely because it lacks the inquisitorial edge that tends to arouse defensiveness in a client. So I will try to keep a space open for Kate's self-enquiry, allowing her to reflect in a way that feels natural to her, while attempting to keep her on point.

I look out the window and see the golden light of the evening sun on the brick wall of the building across the street. The light appears warm on the burnt orange brick which makes me feel peaceful – unlike Kate, who is, I suspect, still wrapped up with her anxieties and concerns. Emotional turmoil, rather than meta-reflections on the self and psychotherapy, is what brings most people into therapy, so I doubt that she would have much interest in my end of the day ruminations. But what does Kate make of me? Freud believed that the emotional transactions between patient and analyst will always have their roots in the patient's childhood experience, and rather than lament the fact that childish feelings interfere with the self-insight that therapy attempts to encourage, the analyst should try to recognise and make use of those psychic remnants of the client's childhood. Indeed, according to Freud, the relational dynamic between therapist and client lies at the very heart of psychotherapy. That seems true enough to me, but I have never been quite sure how this actually works in practice. How, I wonder, does Kate regard me as an older male figure, and will she be able to work with me on the deep-seated problem with her father which seems to have contributed to her decision to turn to therapy? These are idle speculations at this point, common enough at the beginning of therapy, which can be answered only in the course of our interactions. The important thing, I believe, is to be open to surprise, which means that I will be keeping my musings in the background as I get to know her. Besides, it has always seemed to me that sensitivity to context, and alertness to mood, are more valuable than idle speculation,

I am the last one to leave the building and so it is left to me to lock up. The place where I work accommodates a number of different therapists, including acupuncturists, herbalists. massage therapists and other body workers. It is a pleasant, rather soothing environment during office hours, but now that the place is empty it feels particularly serene. As I lock the door, I like to imagine that the peace I experience in the building at closing will be there tomorrow when I see other clients. It is a late summer evening and there is still plenty of daylight as I go out and unlock my bicycle for my ride home. I see no one out on the street now and so my thoughts remain on my last session of the day. My bike ride home, a brisk physical activity which contrasts pleasantly with the mental labour of psychotherapy, still leaves me in my thoughts. Why have I become a therapist? The work is often inconclusive and sometimes frustrating, and it isn't really lucrative for me, either. But I am fascinated by my work and have never done anything as meaningful as practising as a psychotherapist. I still often wonder: am I actually helping the people I see? I used to think that there was a special sort of person who possesses all the attributes for practising therapy through some sort of inheritance or karmic disposition. If there are such people, I haven't met them, and I am certainly not one of them myself. Always fallible, I have to learn as I go along. Even so, I take satisfaction in knowing that I have sometimes been able to help people in their often painful attempts to find their truth. But what the truth was for each of them began as an unknown, as a mystery, in fact, just as it is for Kate, and as it is for me. I am already looking forward to our next appointment.

Following the Money Mindfully

Suzy was a smart, attractive professional in her mid-forties who suffered from periodic bouts of depression which made her believe that her apparently successful life was actually a wretched failure. When she fell into depression Suzy could spend an entire weekend barely able to raise her head above her duvet to get out of bed. This would have been difficult for the people who worked with her to believe. Not only did she seem to succeed effortlessly in the investment banking firm she worked for, she had also gained a reputation for being highly competent without being abrasive, a tricky balancing act which is demanded far more often of women than men. Clever and witty, Suzy managed to leaven her otherwise daunting reputation for competence with a reassuring talent for gentle humour. If there was any indication to others of her unhappiness it might have been in her love life, though not because she lacked suitors. To paraphrase Groucho Marx, Suzy refused to accept anyone who would want her as a partner. As a result, any relationship that she had was always short lived, even when she consented to being in one. But she didn't come to see me about the absence of love in her life. She was resigned to that, or so she said. She was convinced her true problem was one of self-management.

Suzy came to see me on the recommendation of a friend of hers who suggested that I was unusual as a psychotherapist in being so openly Buddhist. In fact, I like to think of myself as quietly Buddhist and in practice not much different from any other responsible therapist. But she was intrigued by my training in Buddhist psychology so I explained to her that while I did use some Buddhist ideas such as *avidya* [ignorance] and *trishna* [craving] to understand negative emotions, I made it clear that these mostly served my spiritual and philosophical interests and that I had no interest in converting anyone to my religious beliefs.

"Then you won't be teaching me to meditate or chant or anything like that?" she asked in a faintly teasing tone.

"No", I said, rather amused. "Those things can be very useful. But it's not the way I work."

"So how *do* you work?"

"I listen and try to reflect with you", I replied.

"Oh", she said, feigning disappointment. "Like any other therapist, you mean."

"Pretty much", I admitted. "But did you come here hoping to become enlightened or something?"

"Well, no", she said, and appeared to enjoy my own teasing. "But I was hoping that you might have something I could use when I need it."

"You mean some sort of technique?"

"Well, yes; you know, something practical. Something that I can use when things get really desperate."

"Like a mantra?" I wondered aloud.

"No, not that!" she cried in mock horror "I would try TM if I wanted that. I just want something that will help me keep calm in times of stress."

"Right", I said, beginning to pick up her drift. "You must be thinking of mindfulness. But when do you find yourself in stress?"

"Well, when I am down, almost always."

"So when do you get down?" I asked, perhaps a bit too inquisitively.

"You really are like any other therapist", she said, deftly fending off my question.

Although I didn't know what ideas Suzy had about mindfulness, I was quite sure that they were not the same as mine. Because of the recent enthusiasm for secular mindfulness as an all-purpose therapeutic intervention, people tend to think that Buddhism is largely about meditation and believe that Buddhists sail serenely through life no matter what conditions of stress they face. Mindfulness, as I know from my own personal experience, really can be helpful in reducing stress and I wouldn't hesitate to recommend it to almost anyone, provided that the teacher is competent and sensitive to the needs of the individual asking for instruction. But not even the Buddha regarded mindfulness as a panacea, and he insisted that it must be linked to morality and wisdom before its benefits could be fully realised.

Moreover, if used unskilfully, mindfulness can actually make a person's problems worse. Given what she told me, I suspected that what Suzy really wanted was a simple mental technique that would give her instant tranquillity. She seemed less interested in the self-examination that psychotherapy calls for, which often requires a potentially painful investigation into one's actual life experience. So, after her first appointment I wasn't sure that we had made a promising beginning, even though we parted on a pleasant note. I even thought she might be better off with a more cognitive approach like CBT that would incorporate mindfulness more seamlessly into its therapeutic regimen. Yet, mindfulness can have an important place in psychotherapy, as in other forms of therapy. It is just a question of what is meant by being mindful.

Mindfulness was first recorded as an instruction of the Buddha in the *Satipatthana Sutta* in the oldest collection of Buddhist teachings, the Pali Canon. The text advises a monk to find a quiet place such as a cave or at the root of a tree and settle into a comfortable sitting position and begin to focus attention on the breath. As thoughts and feelings arise, the monk should simply observe them without being ensnared by craving or interest. While the text praises mindfulness in the highest terms as "the true path to *nibbanna* [nirvana]", it is hard to see how such a transcendent result could follow from such humble means. For there are no references to miracles, no divine interventions and no otherworldly manifestations. The teaching simply calls for contemplation of ordinary reality, not in order to find some hidden, supernatural layer of experience, but to observe the play of mental activity that inexorably follows from craving. The practice does not end in mere self-observation, however. As the monk witnesses the cessation of those cravings which cause his sense of self to arise, he is in an advantageous position to make a profound discovery: when all desires fade, the experience of self fades along with them. According to Buddhism, once this discovery is made, a monk is on the path to nirvana, lasting freedom from suffering.

It is worth noting that the *Satipatthana Sutta* is addressed to monks, though there is no prohibition for non-monastics to undertake the practice. Still, the text assumes that whoever takes up mindfulness will do so in a spirit of uncompromising dedication and ignore the pleasures, distractions and woes of the world. Even so, throughout Buddhist history, lay people have used mindfulness to deal with worldly stress. In Thailand, for example, going into a monastery and taking temporary monastic vows is a common way of dealing with personal misfortune. But Buddhism has always maintained that the world is fraught with danger and temptation, and in order to find final emancipation and escape from *samsara*, the cycle of birth and death, complete renunciation of worldly interests is an essential requirement. This is quite different from secular mindfulness which advertises its benefits in almost entirely practical or worldly terms. Promising to make us better workers, students, parents, and even warriors and lovers, secular mindfulness seldom questions the value of manifestly worldly endeavours.

While some Buddhist teachers see secular mindfulness as a positive development that can lead people to embrace more spiritual values, others see it as a serious dilution of the Buddha's teaching. However it is seen, secular mindfulness has proven to be a fairly effective way of reducing stress for a variety of psychological and physical conditions, so there is good reason for therapists to use it. The question is how to put it to use, especially as a tool for psychotherapy. There is a danger of what Jack Kornfield, a psychotherapist and former Buddhist monk, calls "spiritual bypassing", of using mindfulness to retreat into pleasant, mildly blissful mental states in order to avoid dealing with past traumas or difficulties arising in one's personal life. Mindfulness has proven particularly compatible with a cognitive based approach like CBT, as both mindfulness and CBT cultivate a sense of detachment from the anxieties and concerns that cause stress. CBT targets stress therapeutically in line with its ideas of mental health, whereas mindfulness as a spiritual practice aims for total self-transcendence. Even so, both approaches regard the idea of self as an obstacle to be surmounted rather than as a fundamental existential concern. Psychotherapy, by contrast, regards the self as a primary source of personal meaning, and mindfulness isn't used as a meditative technique to eliminate stress as in CBT, or find the truth of not-self as in Buddhist meditation. If mindfulness has a place in psychotherapy, it is by becoming aware of the unconscious influences of desire and aversion that feed into intentional actions.

Suzy herself had little patience for introspection and regarded it as little more than a pointless self-indulgence. I was somewhat surprised by this as she could be ironic and perceptive, especially when she was discussing the intrigues and rivalries in her place of work. Yet, her insights were always situationally bound, and she had little inclination to consider things from a deeper, more personal perspective. As she admitted, her work had become her life, and rather than pine for some more pleasant alternative she wanted to make the best out of her present situation until the next phase of her life came along. I wondered what she thought the next phase of her working life might be.

"I don't know. Consultancy perhaps. My work experience is bound to be valuable to somebody", she said.

"But would it be rewarding to you?" I asked.

"It could be. It would all depend on the rewards."

"Which would have to be financial?"

"Of course!" she said archly. "It's the way we keep score, you know."

"So do you keep score that way, too?"

"Doesn't everybody? Everybody except you Buddhists, I suppose."

I had to smile at Suzy's gentle mockery. But I was more intrigued by her use of the phrase 'keeping score', which, while a common enough expression in the business and financial worlds in which she worked, seemed to rank highly in her mind as a measure of her self-worth.

"So who's the scorekeeper?" I asked, pursuing the point further.

"Well, I am, of course. Who else?"

"Right", I said, if only to confirm the obvious. Given her professional success, the question then was why, especially in the throes of depression, did she so often score herself a failure.

*****

Before leaving university, Suzy never imagined going into the financial world. As a teenager she had even imagined that she would be an artist ("Except that I wasn't very good", she said with a laugh). At university she read history and obtained a First, but it was a certain extracurricular talent that led to the discovery of her true metier. Suzy was a shrewd judge of other people, perceptive not only about their personalities and talents, but also of the way they would interact with each other. For this reason, she usually wound up organising parties and other social events among her circle of friends, and the ease and skill with which she made such arrangements earned their affection and admiration. It also opened the door for her when she went to look for work in the City of London after university. Although she wasn't sure what skills she could claim in applying for a job in Human Resources in a major firm, her friends who helped her land an interview had no doubts about her abilities at all. They were right. She got the job and quickly advanced through a succession of well-paid positions as she proved highly competent in a number of different roles.

"And that pleased you?" I asked.

"Well, yes, of course, I was pleased."

"So when did you start experiencing depression?"

"Oh that? Well, when haven't I?"

Actually, Suzy's first serious depressive episode occurred during a summer break from university. She had just broken off from a relationship that she had been having, but she was certain that heartbreak wasn't the reason. She claimed her relationship hadn't been all that serious and the split with her boyfriend was fairly amicable. What she considered more significant was that she had always felt there was some depressive tendency lurking beneath her appearance of cheerful insouciance. When depression did eventually settle over her it felt like a fog drifting in from the sea, and it seemed strangely familiar to her. Yet, there was little in her family background or early life experience that seemed to indicate her propensity for depression. Her family, which included both her parents and a brother and sister, was stable, middle class and had high, though attainable, expectations of success. Suzy admitted that apart from her solicitor father's expression of his staunch Tory views, her family was not particularly demonstrative. "No pouting allowed in my family", she said. "It was all stiff upper lip." Not that she disapproved, either. "I think it made me self reliant so I can hardly complain." But none of this explained what made her prone to depression.

Finding cause for any psychological condition is not always an easy or straightforward matter as there can be any number of influences that contribute to the formation of a personality. Apart from an obvious trauma, things like physical health, social, interpersonal and environmental factors can all play a part. There are other, harder-to-detect influences, as well. Yet, there is an increasing tendency among mental health professionals to minimise the factors that make up a person's experience to focus on the symptoms of the client's condition, instead. Mild chronic depression, for example, is now termed dysthymia and is often treated with antidepressants, perhaps along with some CBT or counselling thrown in for good measure. Such a pragmatic, problem-solving approach can certainly provide relief for some people. But for others, keeping the door to the great cavernous mystery of the self firmly closed seems only to limit their anxiety without actually coming to terms with it.

At first, Suzy was happy to use coping strategies she learned from self-help books and she had become fairly adept at using them. She had also taken antidepressants during particularly stressful periods of her life. But her lingering sense of unease and occasional lapses into fog-like depression made her wonder if she could address her problem at its source. But where exactly was the source? A central principle of Freudian psychoanalysis is that the deepest roots of anyone's personality are to be found in early infantile and childhood experience, and most other schools of psychotherapy would agree. Exploring the past through personal memories is an important part of therapy, which is less a matter of making a perfectly coherent narrative from infancy than it is of finding the influence of memory in the construction of current experience. Although Suzy didn't like to think about the past, or as she preferred to put it, didn't like to "wallow" in it, she reluctantly came to accept that we would have to talk about the important things in her early life. But she made her past sound so completely ordinary that she sounded rather bored talking about it.

I learned that her father could be grumpy and that her mother was a tidy and efficient housekeeper. She got along well with her two older siblings, a brother and a sister who were pleasant, sensible people who seemed to be doing well for themselves in adulthood, though Suzy was seldom in touch with them now. But then, she hadn't been particularly close to them when she was growing up, either. Fortunately, she had been able to avoid loneliness as a child through her knack for making friends. But her friendships tended to come and go, and she wasn't sure she could identify anyone as a close, lifelong friend. The same pattern of forming brief emotional ties carried over into her adult relationships with men. Her first romance occurred when she was at university, which she regarded as little more than a rite of passage. But in her twenties, and starting out in her career, her love life became rather adventurous. Those were days of working hard and playing hard, of champagne, cocaine and rich, casual lovers who drove expensive sports cars. But had she ever been seriously committed to anyone?

"Only once", she said rather flatly.

"Who was he?"

"A colleague."

"And?"

"And nothing, really. I think work got in the way. It always had a way of doing that."

"Did you break off the relationship, or did he?"

"I think we both did. It wasn't as if we had a massive row or anything. It just became apparent to both of us that it wasn't going to last."

"How did that affect you?"

"Well, it didn't break my heart, if that's what you're getting at", she said with a trace of annoyance.

"I didn't mean to suggest anything. I was just wondering what your reaction was."

"Somewhat relieved, actually."

What was most revealing about Suzy's recollections was less their content, than the way she discussed them. She was evasive, ironic and reluctant to admit that there had been much emotion invested in anything she did. It was clear that she was driven and ambitious, and had had to summon considerable energy and resources to succeed in her career. Though she was well rewarded financially, as she got older she suffered a certain barrenness in her emotional life which she felt most deeply in her bouts of depression. But Suzy didn't see the connection between the barrenness of her emotional life and the demands placed on her by her professional career.

Perhaps, I mused to myself, it was the way she kept score, confusing financial success with emotional satisfaction. If so, it was a common enough error, indeed it was virtually a culturally shared delusion which took such a powerful hold on her precisely because it seemed so sensible, even commonsensical to her. Countering such a widely held cultural belief is always difficult, but it's particularly hard if it becomes a central factor in someone's self-understanding. Yet, understanding it is not a matter of engaging in some form of social criticism; it's a matter of encouraging the client to look within.

"Mind precedes all mental states. Mind is their chief; they are all mind wrought", begins the Dhammapada, a classic Buddhist text which distils the basic ideas of Buddhism. But the Buddhist concept of mind is not quite the same as the ordinary understanding of the term. Indeed, there are at least three different terms for mind in Buddhist psychology, which correspond roughly to the functions of consciousness, subjectivity and perception. A feature that unites all these separate functions is *trishna*, which is usually translated as craving, and indicates the driven, dynamic nature of the mind in quest of what it perceives as its needs. These features of mind combine to create a sense of self that is ruled by craving without much recognition of the fact. Much like the Freudian ego, which acts without being fully aware of its motivations, the self as conceived by Buddhism is constituted by cravings which remain largely concealed. Yet, we typically regard ourselves as stable in our self-orientation and are unable to see how limited our self-understanding is. It is as if we are asleep to our deepest urges and only become aware of them when our slumber becomes disturbed. The point of therapy, whether Buddhist or not, is to help the client wake up.

One of the things that began to puzzle me about our work together was why Suzy continued to come to see me when she so often expressed doubts about what therapy was doing for her. Though voiced in a characteristically ironic tone, she often made it seem that seeing me once a week was little more than a self-indulgence. For my part, I wasn't sure that anything useful was happening in our interactions either. But I also knew that even when therapy seems to be going nowhere it can still be working subliminally if the therapist is able to remain attentive and engaged. So when Suzy came in and did little more than rehash routine events from her work, I was careful to stay focussed on the apparently trivial matters she brought forward, in the hope that she would eventually bring something that would offer an opening into her intentional actions. As so often happens, it came through a realisation she made about therapy itself.

"I have finally worked out why I keep coming back to see you", Suzy said one day when she looked somewhat brighter than usual.

"Oh?"

"Yes. You make me see how boring I am."

"But I never suggested you were boring, did I?"

"No. But I realise now that I just waffle on when I talk to you."

"What makes you say that?"

"Because every week I just come here and say basically the same things. The events and people I talk about may change, but it's always just the same old nonsense."

"Nonsense?"

"Nonsense because I don't like what I am doing but still keep doing it."

"So what should you be doing instead?"

"It's your job to come up with a solution, isn't it?" she said teasingly.

"To tell you what to do? Certainly not."

"Then what am I doing here?" she asked impishly.

"You tell me."

After this session we did actually begin to have more substantive discussions. She began to see that her attachment to work had a compulsive quality which she had previously attributed to external pressures. And her outlook did improve as she began to feel that she was gaining more insight into the beliefs and intentions that supported her moods. At this point she began to speak more favourably about therapy, as she could see the practical benefits of finding more clarity about her emotional life. But after a while she decided that she didn't need therapy any more. In our final session, Suzy declared that our work together had been a success.

I had doubts about the depth of her transformation, though I didn't express my reservations to her. In my view, there was still much that she could have explored, particularly about the pattern of her relationships, and I wasn't convinced that her new found sense of stability would last. But I kept my doubts to myself, and said that if she ever felt a need to talk to me again she should feel free to call me.

Almost a year later she rang for an appointment.

As soon as Suzy walked into my consulting room I could see a change in her appearance. Though still stylish and attractive, she was also thinner and seemed to have aged noticeably, as well. More subtle, though perhaps more revealing, was the change in her eyes. They no longer seemed to move and take in her surroundings with their former alertness, but seemed strangely fixed and inexpressive. Quite simply, she looked far more depressed than I had ever known her. I couldn't help but wonder what had happened since I had last seen her. After welcoming her back and exchanging the usual pleasantries, I raised the inevitable question.

"So what brings you here again?"

"I am not sure. I thought perhaps talking to you again would be good for me."

"Did something happen?"

"Not really. The fog seems to be rolling in again. It all seems oddly familiar, yet disorienting, too."

"Has anything happened to you that might have triggered this?" I asked.

"No. Nothing has really happened; nothing at all."

Though her appearance suggested otherwise, I was not about to dispute her claim. I didn't doubt her sincerity, but I did wonder about the accuracy of her self-appraisal. Nothing terrible or traumatic may have happened to her, yet something must have occurred, even if she couldn't identify what it was. For my part, I wondered about the fog of depression that was rolling in, for this was a happening, albeit of a vague, nebulous kind.

"So can you remember when you started to notice you were depressed?" I asked.

"Not really. I suppose it was when I didn't seem to have any feelings at all. I felt nothing: literally nothing."

"You mean you experienced a feeling of nothingness?"

"Yes, a feeling of nothingness. That's it exactly. Not quite dead, but not really alive, either."

When people complain about feelings of nothingness it is usually taken as a sign of depression. Indeed, many depressed people do suffer from feelings of nothingness or emptiness, mostly because of their inability to make any meaningful connection with other people. The poet Philip Larkin captured this mood perfectly with a line in his sombre masterpiece, *Aubade*: "...nothing to love or link with, the anaesthetic from which none come round." Suzy was reluctant to talk about the lack of love in her life, but her absence of feeling about almost everything suggested a deeply buried frustration. Her fog of depression didn't come in off the sea; it came from a chain of feeling that was active, yet hidden from her – that is to say, it was unconscious. How to make an unconscious source of suffering conscious has always been the great task of psychotherapy. Yet doing this is seldom easy or straightforward. There is, however, a simple piece of advice that usually yields rewards.

Trace the line of desire, or, to put it into mildly ironic terms that Suzy would readily appreciate, follow the money.

Suzy's financially rewarding career did in fact come at a steep price.

Her once adventurous love life had become virtually non-existent, and her social life had become little more than a series of perfunctory engagements associated with work. She seldom saw members of her family, either. She spent most of her free time alone, watching television or reading what she described as "trashy chick-lit novels". Losing oneself by killing time in mindless activity is common enough, but the idle pleasures people turn to often reveal their deeper passions. I wondered then if there was any deeper significance of such books for her emotional life. Certainly she was far more inclined to remain home reading about such romances than actually having them herself. Yet at one time she actually did have an exciting love life, so I wondered what she found in such pallid substitutes.

"It's just escapism, that's all", Suzy said breezily.

"Yes, I can see that. But why are you escaping that way?" I persisted.

"I don't know. I suppose I'm just shallow."

"I wouldn't say so. But I still have to wonder if somehow those books aren't expressing some unfulfilled need."

"For what?"

"That's what I'm wondering."

"You don't mean love, do you?"

"Not necessarily. Besides, I'm not sure what that word means to you."

"I'm not sure either."

Inviting clients to reflect on the nature of love can be unwise as it can take them away from a more focussed self-examination. But in Suzy's case the move seemed justified as it encouraged her to reflect on her past with a sense of open enquiry, rather than muse on it with ready-made irony. She began to speak frankly in a serious tone I hadn't heard in her before. It turned out that her adventurous love life was not quite as glamorous as she had made it seem. Her casual lovers tended to be selfish, unfeeling men with little true interest in her. But then, she admitted, she had little real interest in them, either. They simply came together in seemingly uncomplicated liaisons that were supposed to be mutually enjoyable, but which seldom worked out that way. Some could be real bastards, she recalled, though she admitted she had used those men for pleasure or social advantage as much as they used her. But I wondered about the one relationship that might have been serious for her, the man she once considered marrying.

"Tony? Well, yes, he was different."

"How so?"

"I don't know. He was more caring, I suppose. Though I think he might have been too caring for me."

"Was there something wrong with that?"

"No, not in itself. It's just that what he wanted didn't really fit in with what I wanted."

"What did he want?"

"Family, children, a happy home, the lot. But I had too many commitments for that."

"You mean work?"

"Yes, it's always been work", she said with a sigh. "But he was the one who finally decided to end it."

"Why?"

"It was just the choice he felt he had to make."

"But what was his reason?"

"He wanted more of me than I was willing to give, I suppose. And to be quite honest, I just couldn't see myself giving up the life I had", she said rather defensively.

"Do you ever regret your decision?"

"Not really. Besides, there isn't much point, especially now."

"Maybe not. But you still might regret it."

"I don't think I would have let myself feel that."

"So you've stopped yourself from feeling it?"

"Yes. It's one of the things I'm rather good at. Self-discipline, you know."

"Do you have any feelings for Tony now?"

"No, not any more. I haven't thought of him in years until your question brought him up. He was sweet, though."

Suzy fell into an uncomfortable silence which did little to conceal her agitation. I remained quiet, too. Naturally, I still wondered what she was thinking, but her facial expression indicated that she wasn't quite ready to speak. When she did eventually speak, the long silence proved worth the wait.

"I never thought I could have it all", she said, at last. "I always knew that if I tried to get one thing, it would mean that I might have to sacrifice something else. But I always thought that if I got the thing I was aiming for, I would be satisfied."

"And is that what happened?"

"Do you think I would be here if it had?" she replied, the softness of her voice not quite concealing her annoyance at my question. "Actually, I now realise I didn't want just one thing. I wanted two – independence, as well as love. Now I'm not even sure what either of those things mean."

Although therapists often discuss psychotherapy in terms of healing, describing it in this way can be misleading. Still, metaphors of psychological wounding and healing are almost irresistible as psychological pain can be as unbearable and as lasting as any physical injury. But a psychological wound is an actual phenomenon that endures only because it recurs in experience and becomes a lasting affliction because letting it go seems both impossible and intensely desirable. Psychological wounds are actually thoughtless reactions, or mindless, unconscious ways of being that originate as defences against psychological pain, but become sources of pain themselves. Being ruled by a process of unconscious avoidance, a person becomes haunted by the very things she is trying to escape.

When the Buddha taught mindfulness, he taught far more than a way of pacifying the mind. His teaching included his ideas on ethics and spiritual development, as well. But seeing things as they really are – impermanent, not-self and suffering – has always been the essence of his teaching. In this spirit, he advised his followers to confirm for themselves the truths that he taught. Although psychotherapy should never be used to preach Buddhism, it can encourage the clear self-awareness that comes from being mindful of the impermanent nature of existence, and of the deceptiveness inherent in self-experience.

Therapeutic mindfulness can help dispel the evasions, the self-deceptions and the harmful illusions that keep us stuck in self-defeating patterns of suffering. But therapy cannot offer a path of final liberation to nirvana that the Buddha indicated when he taught mindfulness. It can only offer the more modest liberation of finding another, better way to live. For most of us, this usually proves to be enough.

Suzy's change was slow and hesitant, as so often happens in therapy. Though she could still experience a fog of depression, she was able to see that it mostly rolled in on her days off when she was alone. Even better, she grew increasingly confident that her depressive moods wouldn't last forever, and she came to expect that they would fade away much as they had come on. But I wondered if managing her depression was all that she could hope for. The greatest rewards from therapy come from insights that make meaningful change possible. Still, all a therapist can do is provide a space for reflection and meaningful encounter, both of which allow such realisations to take place. Eventually, Suzy left therapy again, not with the cheerfulness and high confidence of her previous departure, but with modest thanks and a quiet farewell. Although she didn´t rule out resuming therapy at some point in the future, she felt that she had had enough for the time being.

I heard from Suzy a couple of years later when she sent me a letter. She was now living with a partner, someone she had known at university who was practising as a GP. She was still working, but at a far less demanding job. She also had some new ideas about how she would spend her retirement. She was no longer interested in becoming a business consultant, and she thought she might offer her skills to a charity, instead. She believed that therapy was helpful to her, though she couldn't say quite how. What she really found helpful was the sitting meditation that she practised every day. She thought that since I was a Buddhist, I would be pleased to hear it.

Love and Death

Although psychotherapy is an extraordinarily intimate form of communication, as a rule I avoid saying too much about my personal life to my clients. Therapy should always be focused on the experience of the client, and there is a danger of losing focus by allowing it to shift, however temporarily or innocently, to the therapist. For this reason, some therapists are extremely guarded in dealing with their clients and may regard even small talk about their personal lives as a distraction from the therapeutic interaction. Others are like me and don't mind revealing unimportant facts about themselves so long as these disclosures don't detract from the client's need to remain engaged in his own therapeutic process. But I suspect many therapists would be reluctant to discuss what most of us regard as an important truth: we would have little hope of understanding the personal experiences of our clients without drawing on similar personal experiences of our own. This is not so much a tightly held professional secret as it is a quietly understood truth. Of course, no one's personal experience is so extensive that he will always have something from his past to draw on for immediate therapeutic purposes. But by reflecting on his past experience, a therapist can use his memory as a resource that contributes to his understanding of what his clients are going through. The past of the therapist is as alive as the past of the client, and in some way, it is through the convergence of the memories of both parties that psychotherapy finds a fertile common ground.

When I first met George, a retired teacher who came to see me because of his unremitting grief over the unexpected death of his wife, I immediately thought of my mother. There was an obvious reason for this as I had a vivid memory of witnessing her grieve when my father died almost twenty years before George suffered his own loss. As I listened to George struggle to express his feelings, I had a strong sense that I knew what he was going through, as I had seen almost the same thing in my mother. I happened to be visiting my parents when my father died and I have a vivid memory of witnessing the shock that she felt. He died in the middle of the night after a pleasant evening which gave no warning that he was going to die later on. I was asleep when my mother burst into my bedroom and urged me to wake up. "It's Dad!" my mother screamed. "He's having a heart attack!" I called an ambulance and, though untrained in CPR, I made a feeble attempt to revive him. But by the time the ambulance arrived my father had crossed the threshold into irreversible brain damage, and his conscious life had come to its end. The EMS crew asked me if I wanted them to save him, but knowing that he would not have wanted to survive in such a vegetative state, I spared my mother any role in making such a painful decision. I told them to let him die. I have never regretted my choice and my mother was in fact grateful to me for making it. Yet, at the moment after the ambulance crew left and the undertakers had come to take away my father's corpse, I had never seen her look so vulnerable and alone. "I don't know how I can live without him", she said, appearing too afraid to weep. Later, her tears did flow freely, but what has always stayed in my memory from that moment was how throttled her expression of grief was. It was as if she wanted to explode with sorrow but feared that if she surrendered to the impulse she might never emerge from her overwhelming sadness.

George appeared to need to overcome a natural reticence in order to express his emotions to a stranger like me. I learned that he had been encouraged to seek therapy by his daughter, Rose, who knew that, almost a year after her mother's death from cancer, he was still mired in grief. Instead of enjoying his usual pastimes of reading, walking and working in his garden, he mostly sat alone in an armchair, gazing at the television without really watching it. He also had difficulty sleeping and he seemed to have lost his appetite too. At first, he had gone to his GP who prescribed antidepressants, but he found they only made him feel worse and eventually he refused to take them. Afterwards, Rose convinced him that it might be helpful to talk to someone and, as so often happens in therapy, he came to see me because of a recommendation from a friend of hers. He was eighty-four, a tall man with a slight stoop, who walked with a slow, shuffling gait. Though polite, he was not particularly forthcoming in replying to my questions. But it didn't take long before I realised that he was sitting on a powerful feeling.

"So what brings you here?" I asked him directly.

"I'm not sure," he replied. "But my daughter thought it might be good if I spoke to someone."

"But what about you? Do you think I might be able to help you?"

"Maybe you can", he said cautiously. "But I don't really know what you can do."

"Maybe it would be good to begin by telling me what you have been feeling", I suggested gently. His response caught me by surprise.

"I have been..." he began before he suddenly stopped, apparently overcome with emotion. His initial reaction led me to expect that some outburst, possibly involving tears, would soon follow. But then he suddenly held back, like someone who was about to cough out a ball of phlegm and just managed to choke it back. He then looked at me as if he had narrowly avoided a *faux pas* and seemed to be silently imploring me not to question him about what I had just witnessed. As it was only our first meeting, I felt it was only right to respect his need to save face, and I paused for a moment to let him compose himself before I resumed speaking. We both seemed to abide by the pretence that his suppressed emotion was only a contained cough. But in the back of my mind, I remembered my mother in her moment of acute grief.

"You were married for a long time. How long were you married?" I asked.

"Fifty-one years", George replied in a strong, clear voice. His simple, factual reply seemed to steady him. It also encouraged him to reminisce and he soon began to talk more freely about his life with Doris.

Most of us have prepared narratives about ourselves for others to hear. Although our stories may be more or less true, they are usually self-serving, and at least in psychotherapy, they should seldom be taken at face value. But one fact seemed consistent throughout George's self-narrative, and I had little reason to doubt it. He had been a strong and devoted husband and Doris could always rely on him to manage things for her. Moreover, it was a role that was central to his identity. But now that he was a widower he felt bewildered by both the death of Doris and the loss of his role. The expression that when his wife died a part of him died, too, was no cliché for him. He actually felt her absence as a palpable sense that an essential part of him was irretrievably lost. Once again, I was able to draw on my memory of my mother's experience to understand what he was going through. Like George, she had taken her marriage to be permanent – indeed, virtually eternal – so that when she lost my father it had seemed unthinkable. Like any self-aware adult she knew that death is an inevitable fact of life, as George surely knew, as well. Yet in the critical moment when this universal truth became actualised in her personal experience, she was racked by disbelief. It seems many of us would suffer a similar shock in dealing with the death of someone they love. Though we all readily admit that death is inevitable for us all, when someone close to us dies we may still find the loss bewildering and unacceptable.

Whenever I hear of an unacceptable death, I always think of the story of Gisa Kotami from the Pali Canon, the oldest scriptures of Buddhism. The story tells of a woman driven mad by grief over the loss of her infant, who begs the Buddha to bring her baby back to life. The Buddha listens to Gisa sympathetically before asking her to bring him a mustard seed from every household in her village that had not been touched by death. It was a fool's errand, of course, but it served a benign and instructive purpose. After going to each house, she finds that no household had been spared bereavement, and she begins to understand that her loss is not exceptional. After this realisation, she then receives instruction from the Buddha on meditation and how to deal with the impermanence of life. Closing on a note of uplift and reassurance, the parable goes on to say that Gisa later attained enlightenment.

Unlike Jesus, the Buddha performs no miracle of raising a child from the dead. Instead, gently and skilfully, he makes her face the painful reality of impermanence, a mystery of which only enlightened spiritual teachers seem to have an adequate understanding. Lacking such an enlightened perspective, we are apt to regard the death of someone we love as an intolerable deprivation. Like Gisa Kotami – and like George and my mother – we might feel that we had lost our reason for living. The question, then, is how to go on living?

George had no difficulty in acknowledging the loss that he felt, but he found it almost impossible to deal with Doris's absence. My mother felt the same way about my father. "This wasn't supposed to happen!" she would often wail. She thought that she and my dad would have another ten or twenty more years together, during which they would remain physically healthy and mentally sound before they would pass away together, presumably in a state of abiding peace. The fact that George and my mother had both enjoyed long marriages well into old age seemed to count for nothing for either of them once they lost their partners. Indeed, it seemed to make their bereavements worse, as they were both unable to imagine ever feeling better. In fact, intense grief closely resembles depression, so much so that there is a debate as to whether grief should be regarded as a form of depression if it continues for more than two months after the loss that provoked it.

The debate may never be settled, as the various factors involved in grief can be complex and aren't readily appreciated from a medical point of view alone. Moreover, the profound shift of mood that happens when someone's grief eventually lifts can be difficult to predict. It seems to be more of an occurrence than a willed action, though doing some things and avoiding others can ease the oppressive sense of loss. One of the most helpful things a therapist can do is to allow the client to reflect on his loss and offer him an opportunity to make sense of his conflicted feelings. For George, this happened by reflecting on a recurrent dream.

At first, George seemed reluctant to explore his dreams, as he found them confusing and difficult to remember. What he *did* remember he often found unpleasant, as well as nonsensical. But then something unexpected emerged as he began to recall his dreams more clearly. He had a recurring dream, which unsurprisingly featured Doris. But it also included his mother, a feature that did surprise him. In the dream, both his wife and mother were in a train station like Kings Cross in London before its recent renovation, waiting for him to pick them up. He could see them both clearly, but they couldn't see him, as he was standing in a crowd of people and was barred from going up to where they stood. At this point in the dream, he would always wake up, frustrated by his inability to reach them.

The meaning of his dream was obvious in one sense – George missed Doris and longed to be reunited with her. More puzzling was the presence of his mother in his dream, for Doris's relationship with her had always been troublesome. In fact, George's own relationship with his mother had always been difficult for reasons that were still painful for him to recall. His father had been killed in WWII, leaving his mother alone with George and his younger sister when they were small children. He supposed that losing her husband in the war must have come as a terrible blow to her. Moreover, his mother never remarried or had a close relationship with anyone else. Still, her loss didn't entirely explain why she was so often unaccountably moody and sullen, or explain why she would often lash out over petty annoyances with frightening suddenness. It seemed likely to me that his mother had been depressed, though I didn't express this idea to George. The more important question was how his experience of his mother had affected him, the riddle at the heart of his recurrent dream which seemed to invite an interpretation. I found one almost irresistible, which seemed to explain why the dream placed his mother next to his wife. The love that he was unable to obtain from his mother as a child was being thwarted again by the death of Doris. Although George thought my interpretation might have some merit, his thoughts travelled on a different and more promising track.

Usually polite and reserved in his greeting, George came in one day and gave me a rather perfunctory nod before he sat down in his chair as if to release a burden. Seeing that he had something important to say, I didn't bother to ask a question, but simply waited for him to speak. At first, he didn't look at me at all, but gazed into space for a long moment, apparently to gather his thoughts. When he finally spoke, it had the authority of a revelation.

"I have finally realised something", he said at last. "I will never be with Doris again, but she will always be with me."

"What do you mean?" I asked.

"I mean she's always on my mind, but I will never be able to find her in real life. Whenever I walk into a room I still expect to find her there, even though I know she's gone forever. But I lived for her. She gave me my reason for living. That's just who I was. But now that she's gone it's as if I'm not even alive", he said with uncharacteristic passion.

"You sound almost angry", I observed with surprise.

"I am!" he practically roared. "I know it doesn't make any sense, but I keep blaming her for dying and leaving me here all alone."

I nodded in agreement, for I had heard virtually the same thing from my mother when my father died years before. It was as if Doris's absence weighed on him as much now as her presence did when she was alive. As in his recurring dream, he would always be conscious of Doris while never being able to reach her.

George reached another important insight by reflecting on the feelings evoked by his recurrent dream. It was his realisation that anger was a hidden feature of his grief. This often catches people by surprise as they expect to feel sorrow at the loss of someone they loved, but not anger at the beloved. Whatever anger they expect to feel is reserved for others – an assailant, or a negligent party perhaps – who might be held responsible for the death of the beloved. As for the deceased themselves, they're often enshrined in an aura of eternal goodness, even if they were far from saintly when they were alive. Yet, anger has a stubborn way of intruding into grief and implicating the deceased, no matter how blameless for her death she might have been. As George himself observed, it didn't make any sense to blame Doris for dying of cancer. Yet, at the same time, he felt angry at her for leaving him to live out the rest of his life alone. He felt abandoned, as well as bereaved, and though he could understand his bereavement, he had a more difficult time understanding the anger he felt towards her.

By realising that anger was a component of his grief, George was in a better position to make sense of his feeling of loss. At root, anger is the frustration of desire, and while being angry at Doris for dying made little sense to him, being frustrated at losing his beloved life partner forever made a great deal of sense. In fact, it seemed more than understandable; it appeared entirely natural.

Eventually, George's grief began to subside. It was a gradual process, but his improvement became clear to him once he noticed that he was taking pleasure in the simple things he used to enjoy, such as going out for a walk or pottering in his garden. Even so, he remained aware of the loss of Doris, even in these pleasant activities. Each day, from the moment he woke up, her absence would loom over everything he did. Still, he felt like himself again, and he was no longer overwhelmed by an acute sense of loss. According to one widely held view in psychiatry, George's recovery was largely a biological process of grieving that had simply run its natural course. There was always a strong likelihood it would occur, much like a bodily illness will often remit without medical intervention. Though this view might be correct, as my mother's case proves, nature provides no guarantee for people to come to terms with their bereavements. Many people need emotional support and the opportunity to make sense of their loss, which therapy attempts to provide. Fortunately, therapy was able to meet George's emotional needs and help him recover his sense of self. Even so, losing Doris would remain a defining feature of his experience for the rest of his life.

It's virtually an article of faith for me that deeper self-insight enhances almost everything we do. But how can someone's life be enhanced after losing someone they loved? When George finally ended therapy, there was a rather bittersweet quality to our closure. We shook hands, wished each other well and parted without any expectation that we would meet again. In fact, we never did meet again, as George died almost a year and a half after his last session with me. I suspect he might have even been looking forward to his death, if only to end his sense of loss over Doris. Though not religious, perhaps he even entertained hopes of being reunited with her in the afterlife. After his long life had reached its natural end, his daughter sent me a touching letter informing me that he died peacefully. She expressed appreciation for how much therapy had helped him. For my part, I was pleased that I could draw on my experience of my mother's grief to help George.

My mother never turned to psychotherapy after my father died. Perhaps she would have been more content in her remaining years if she had done so. As it was, she spent her final years living with my sister and her family, and though they provided her with all the love and care they could, she became increasingly withdrawn and more isolated the older she got.

Though the intensity of her grief did abate over time, she was never really able to accept my father's death. She almost seemed to regard his death as a sign that her life was essentially over, until, twenty-three years after his death, it actually was. It seems obvious that she would have been happier if she had adopted a more positive attitude. My sister always believed this, and she often tried to encourage her to get out and socialise more. But my mother ignored her advice and chose to remain in what amounted to perpetual mourning for the remainder of her life.

*****

As an openly Buddhist therapist I am sometimes asked about my beliefs in an afterlife and in reincarnation, but usually I just shrug my shoulders. Although I'm familiar with Buddhism's basic teachings on karma and rebirth, I couldn't begin to advise my clients on any post-mortem reality they might experience. In truth, I am not entirely convinced of an afterlife. Besides, my Buddhist practice is more concerned with cultivating a deeper awareness of this life, not speculating on the possibility of future lives. Yet, there is a certain truth about mortality that can be drawn from working with the bereaved which seems to apply to everyone. To say nothing lasts forever is little more than a cliché; to say everyone must die expresses the same truth, but in more sobering terms. The story of Gisa Kotami goes further and teaches that not even love offers an exemption from the certainty of death. Therapists know how difficult accepting this reality can be by working with clients mourning the loss of someone they loved. But as the parable suggests, such feelings of loss are less about love than they are about attachment.

Love and attachment are not the same thing, of course, though it often seems impossible to tell them apart. Attachment is a form of possession, whereas love is the highest kind of acceptance. For this reason, becoming free of attachments is not the same thing as disavowing love. The Buddhist ideal might even be described as love without attachment, that is to say, of love free of compulsive desire. But even as a Buddhist therapist, I never encourage my clients to abandon their love interests to take up the holy life. If anything, I usually support their attempts to experience love, though I also try to help them become aware of what drives their desire for it. I also try to suggest that love is a matter of becoming more aware of the people they love, of their desires and needs, as well as the truth of impermanence as it applies to the people they care for. Impermanence is what made love so agonising for Gisa Kotami. But in my reading of the parable, she does not regret the love she felt for her child. With the Buddha's guidance, she learns to accept the reality of death and keep her heart open, even after her terrible loss.

Psychotherapy commonly deals with problems that involve love and death, issues which both religion and literature have also taken as two of their most important and enduring themes. Contemplating eternally recurring life events to arrive at psychological insight is one of the most important things that religion and literature do. As a therapist, in fact, I have learned as much about human experience by reflecting on great spiritual and literary texts as I have by reading any books on psychology. But though it shares some interests with literature, psychotherapy is not any sort of literary or religious endeavour. Stories of love and death may offer valuable insights for our own experience, but it is only by experiencing things personally that we discover who we are. In confronting both love and death, we have no choice but to experience ourselves in the first person, in the very skin of our individual being. Therapy can assist in the discovery.

The Kindness of Others

One of the satisfactions I get from being a therapist comes from helping people find greater emotional freedom by developing deeper self-insight. The key discovery a person makes through self-insight is that he is the principal agent of his life, and not a passive victim of his circumstances. By taking responsibility for what he does and thinks, he discovers the freedom to act in accordance with his beliefs and values, even in circumstances he might find difficult or unfavourable. But self-insight is not a stand-alone value, and it should always be linked to the recognition that everyone depends on a modicum of respect and goodwill from others. Ideally, this understanding begins in early childhood and having the good fortune to be raised by loving, caring parents. It will develop further if the child grows up in a supportive and stimulating environment that allows him to explore things freely and securely. From such auspicious beginnings, he will then have the resources to develop a stable sense of self, which is the ideal condition for self-insight to develop. Many people, however, turn to therapy precisely because they lacked the care they needed in childhood to feel secure in their self-development. Whatever self-insight they possess began from a less favourable starting point, usually one characterised by a feeling of deprivation or lack.

Valuable as self-insight is, it can only do so much to compensate for the approval and care they failed to receive as children. Establishing a relationship in which authentic trust becomes a real possibility is essential for working with people who never experienced it as children. For particularly damaged individuals, kindness is even more important than helping them develop self-insight.

Terry was referred to me by a friend of mine, a social worker who knew I was willing to see clients at a reduced fee. A tall, angular man in his late forties, Terry still carried himself with the shy evasiveness of a boy. Although he made an effort to appear friendly and cheerful, it soon became apparent that he carried a crushing emotional burden which affected virtually everything he did. He had been diagnosed with a borderline personality disorder years before he came to see me, and he had been sectioned a number of times for serious acts of self-harm. Social Services had rightly judged him unable to work, and he relied on public assistance to meet his modest material needs. But he felt ashamed of being reliant on the state for his welfare and believed that receiving benefit payments made his pitiful condition plain for the world to see. Unfortunately, given the intensity of his anxiety, which at times could reach a level of acute panic, even the least demanding job had always proved beyond his ability to cope. Yet, he remained convinced that with a more positive attitude he would be able to overcome his anxiety, land a job, and gain some much needed self-respect. His hope was that I would help him find that elusive positive attitude so that he would no longer be cursed with the crippling sense of failure which had dogged him throughout his life.

Helping a client cultivate a positive attitude is by no means out of place in therapy, but for Terry the idea of willpower had become almost a self-defeating obsession. Even so, his efforts at trying to adopt a positive attitude did actually benefit him. He no longer drank alcohol and hadn't harmed himself in several years. It was when he was in the grip of such a despairing mood years before that he had seriously harmed himself, once by slashing his wrists with a broken bottle, and another time by jabbing his thigh repeatedly with a pen knife. But the more common way he used to punish himself was by drinking himself to oblivion, leaving him unable to remember what he had done, but feeling sure it must have been something terrible. Yet, even after overcoming his drinking and self-harming, he still felt as if some mysterious force denied him the normal life that everyone else seemed to enjoy naturally. His faith in the importance of personal responsibility might have been commendable, except that it often left him unable to cope with disappointment, leaving him overwhelmed by a feeling of inadequacy. I wanted to help him, but it seemed he first expected me to regard him with the same disapproval with which he condemned himself. I knew we would need to find a different footing if I could hope to help him at all.

Working with Terry was somewhat difficult at the beginning, even though he was eager to be cooperative and clearly valued my approval. As if by reflex, he blamed himself for almost all his misfortunes, including some that were clearly beyond his control. Moreover, his ideas about therapy were limited by his belief that it should focus solely on self-improvement, and he often expressed doubts about the usefulness of examining his life in any depth.

Fortunately, he was self-aware enough to realise that the roots of his suffering were to be found in his family and childhood experience, and eventually he began to open up about his formative years. The origins of his suffering soon became clear. Terry's parents, whose marriage had always been fractious, had divorced before he began primary school and he had always felt conflicted and even ashamed about their separation. He grew up living with his mother and his disabled younger half-sister, though if he had been given the choice, he would have lived with his father. But his dad was a rootless, impulsive man who had never settled down long enough to take care of Terry. Yet, in spite of his inability to provide for him, Terry's dad was able to express his affection freely, almost ecstatically, and had been able to do something no one else had ever been able to do, before or since. He made Terry feel loved.

Terry cherished one memory of his father that crystallised his feelings about him. He was ten at the time, and his dad, who had been working as a taxi driver, declared he wanted to take him on a camping trip. Against his mother's wishes, his father spirited him away to Devon where they pitched a tent at a cliffside campsite which enjoyed a sweeping view of the sea. He remembered the clean, bracing air of the ocean and the roar of the surf crashing onto the rocky shore below the cliffs. His father was in a particularly ebullient mood and after they made camp and got some fish and chips in a nearby town, he spoke expansively about how well things were going and how he was going to be able to have Terry move in with him at last. Terry might have realised it wouldn't be as easy as his dad had made it sound. Past experience should have told him that his mother would object, and even at his age, he knew his father could exaggerate, making it seem that things he wanted to happen were bound to occur. But as he sat with his dad protected against the chill ocean air by a padded windbreaker and seeing the stars spread out above the Atlantic like diamonds scattered abundantly across the black vault of night, he believed everything that his father told him. It had to be true, he thought, because there was no reason why it shouldn't be. It was as if the universe itself had smiled upon his father's plans with the gentle radiance of starlight, promising happiness because it could be so easily given. It seemed meant to be.

Terry never moved in with his father. Shortly after their return, his father had his driving licence revoked for driving while drunk, and his life went into swift decline. He soon lost his flat and was made homeless, drifting from one place to another as he went searching for another line of work. For a brief time, he even slept on a couch at Terry's home, which might have made Terry happy, except for the bitter arguments which frequently broke out between his parents. Even Terry could see that the blame mostly fell on his dad, as he was often drunk and did little but interfere with the order of the household that his mum tried to maintain. Still, when his father eventually left the house after a particularly heated argument, Terry felt completely gutted. A voice inside his head told him something that would remain with him forever: "I will never see Dad again." Unlike his false revelation in Devon, this prophecy turned out to be true. Two weeks later his father died by drowning after falling into a river while drunk. As he grew older, there would often be times when Terry wished he had drowned with him.

To lose a loving parent in childhood would be a cause of lasting grief for almost anyone, but for Terry the loss of his father was particularly catastrophic. Of all the people he had ever known, only his dad seemed to truly care for him. His mother was dutiful enough about seeing to his bodily needs, but she never expressed any affection for him, or took any interest in his emotional development. His birth was a "bad mistake" she often told him, and made it sound as if the fault was his. And when his mother informed him about his father's death, she showed no sign of sadness or regret. She always knew his dad would die like the fool he was, she said bitterly, and she expressed relief that he wouldn't be coming around to bother her any more. She didn't seem to notice that Terry took the news like a hard blow to his gut. Nor did she show much concern when he began to suffer nightmares and would wake up screaming. She simply yelled at him to shut up because she was trying to sleep. No one ever acknowledged his loss or grief. He also sensed that there would have been something wrong if he had tried to express his feelings to anyone. He felt numb.

A longstanding belief of psychotherapy maintains that if we are not able to express our painful emotions verbally, they will be expressed in some other way, usually with unfortunate consequences. This certainly was the case with Terry. His memory of life after the death of his father was of being like a sleepwalker in a disturbing dream. While everyone else seemed secure in their place in the world, he felt bewildered and unable to communicate his confusion to anyone. He attended school, but he did poorly, and left without qualifications.

Afterwards, in his late teens, he found work in a succession of low paying jobs, but he felt out of place in everything he tried. He never formed friendships or developed his own interests. He just went through the motions of living without feeling truly alive. He did have one island of stability, as he continued to to live with his mother and sister up until his late twenties. But home was mostly a place where he ate, slept and watched television. Still, living there gave him a measure of security, and he never supposed that he might be deprived of it. But when his mother and sister were killed in a car accident, his entire world seemed to cave in on him. He was completely alone now, and even the world that had been familiar to him seemed filled with alien shadows. He started to drink heavily, then lost his job, before he was sectioned for the first time following an incident of harming himself while sitting in a public library. For reasons he couldn't recall, he repeatedly banged his head against a table. The only thing he remembers about that incident was his feeling of utter hopelessness beforehand. Listening to his story, I couldn't imagine how he could have felt any other way.

*****

Sometimes psychotherapy attempts to deal with past traumas by subjecting the memories of those events to sustained though sensitive reflection, but I knew this could be dangerous for someone as fragile as Terry. My main objective was simply to make him feel welcome so that he could talk freely without feeling pressure from me. With other clients, challenging or probing their beliefs and intentions can sometimes prompt them to make a meaningful self-enquiry, but I believed doing this with Terry risked aggravating his acute sense of vulnerability. I didn't even question the feeble excuses he gave when occasionally he came in late, sometimes with only a few minutes to spare before the end of the appointment hour. In fact, I was pleased that he had turned up at all. Later, my patience seemed to pay off as he admitted that when he first came to see me he used to loiter outside on the street, trying to gather the courage to come in. His admission told me that I had finally succeeded in giving him the sanctuary he needed from a world that he often found unbearably hostile. Still, though I was pleased to have been able to make him feel secure and comfortable in my presence, I wasn't sure I would ever be able to do much more for him than this. In fact, we were able to deal with an important matter that contributed to his improvement.

Although Terry's fragile condition ruled out encouraging him to engage in deep introspection, it by no means closed off working with his unconscious processes. If anything, those processes were much closer to the surface of his awareness than they would be for most people, but it made dealing sensitively with Terry an important requirement. For most clients, discovering the life of the unconscious through dream work or active imagination may come as a great revelation. For Terry, the unconscious was like a turbulent sea which not only disturbed his sleep, it also threatened his equilibrium when he was awake. As for waking fantasy, for most people it usually remains safely predictable, turning reliably around familiar themes of desire and aversion. But for Terry, fantasy, especially in times of stress, could be more like an autonomous force that could sweep him away to foreign lands of the unconscious to face terrors that threatened his ability to cope with normal experience. A recurrent reverie of his illustrated this well.

Ever since he was a child, Terry had been subject to disturbing flights of the imagination, which mostly affected him at night before he went to sleep, though such powerful fantasies could also invade his daytime reveries, as well. As an adult living alone, he always went to bed with the radio on to provide some familiar background music to counter the feeling of unease he experienced before falling asleep. Even so, he still couldn't quite eliminate what might be described as the movie in his head, an ongoing stream of imagery and imaginary conversation whose effects could be strikingly cinematic. In fact, we all have such movies in our heads, though we seldom pay much attention to them. Our movies mostly remain unseen, if not entirely unfelt, in the background of our awareness as we engage in ordinary activities. But for Terry, his internal cinema could override all other concerns, especially when he was under great stress. During these periods, he was often visited by an imaginary group of eminent men that he called the Jury. It wasn't quite clear to him who the men that composed the Jury were, but they all wore broad brimmed hats and long cloaks and seemed to belong to some sort of judicial guild from another country and historical era. They gathered together periodically to discuss Terry in tones of grave concern, which made him anxious because he couldn't make out what they were saying and he was unable to tell how they were judging him. Though he knew the scene wasn't real, the vividness of his vision seemed to border on hallucination and made him fear he was losing his hold on reality. Moreover, imaginary or not, he feared the Jury had far more control over his fate than he did.

Dealing with a potent artefact of the unconscious always carries some risk, but it is not always wise to treat it as a symptom of a pathological condition. In Terry's case, he was aware that his recurrent vision of a committee of judges sprang from his imagination, though knowing this seemed to do little to diminish its hold on him. Even though the Jury appeared to exert a powerful influence over him, it wasn't clear what their intentions for him were. It even seemed possible that they might be concerned for his welfare and exerted a stabilising effect on him. I considered it significant that they conducted their meetings with such solemn purpose without being able to reach a decision about him. This seemed to suggest that the Jury expressed much the same indecision that Terry felt about himself. But then, who were these wise men who were deciding his fate? Perhaps they represented various factions of his personality that had taken form in his imagination in order to reach a consensus about his future. Or perhaps they were a quasi-mythological representation of how he felt others were judging him. No matter how his vision was understood, what seemed essential to me was that they should not be given more importance than they deserved. I decided to treat his vision like a dream that expressed an anxiety about his future without supposing that their prophecy would have to come true.

Above all, the apparent autonomy of the Jury should not be allowed to overrule his attempts to find better possibilities for himself. The question then was how to help Terry find a viable sense of self in dealing with this ominous influence from his unconscious.

Observing a dichotomy in experience between an objective outer world and a subjective inner one, though essential for making sense of things, may overlook a crucial third dimension which is especially important for psychotherapy. This is the intersubjective world in which each of us meets the experience of others as they meet ours. It is through intersubjectivity that we encounter each other, not as objects of our experience, but as co-creators and fellow travellers in our shared world of experience. It is this mutual recognition of each other as unique individuals – self-aware, and aware of the self-awareness of others – that discloses the intersubjective realm and enables us to know others as persons like ourselves. Moreover, it is only through intersubjective awareness that we can love, the highest form of relating that people can experience. Yet, intersubjectivity oscillates on the narrow divide between the objective and subjective worlds, and without attention and care, it can easily slip to the margins of awareness. Trust is crucial for maintaining clear intersubjective awareness for therapy and is vital for a therapist to communicate his understanding to the client.

Trying to develop trust with someone as fragile as Terry demanded a great degree of caution which limited what I could say to him. I was tempted, for example, to amplify the effect the Jury had on him by encouraging him to imagine their deliberations to gain some insight into what he thought they were saying about him. But the danger of Terry being overwhelmed by such an imaginary encounter ruled out provoking his imagination, and I had to be careful never to probe his thoughts or moods too forcefully. Thus, everyday topics like football, and what he had watched on television the previous night, featured as often in our conversations as the matters I would have preferred to pursue which were more relevant to his inner condition. Still, I made sure that he knew that I was always ready to discuss these more serious concerns if he ever felt the desire or need to talk about them. I also made it clear that I found his disturbing reveries and seemingly inexplicable anxieties entirely human, if somewhat out of the ordinary. I took it as a sign of success that he did sometimes avail himself of the opportunity to address his more serious concerns. Yet, I was always somewhat frustrated by my inability to probe Terry's inner world more deeply. Fortunately, he had help from other people besides me, and I suspect that it was our combined, though uncoordinated, efforts of supporting him that eventually led to his improvement.

Although psychotherapy does need to provide a sanctuary – a safe space –for clients to come to terms with their experience, it should not attempt to shield them entirely from the harsh realities of the world. Helping them adapt to circumstances that can sometimes be unfair or hostile has always been an important value for therapy, but it should also help them realise that the world is not invariably heartless, either. This entails far more than encouraging a positive outlook. More importantly, it means helping a client recognise and respond to the goodwill of others whenever such kindness appears. Fortunately, a saving grace for Terry was that when he received help from others he truly appreciated it. He had, for example, always expressed gratitude for the help he received from Carol, the social worker who had referred him to me when he was unable to access psychotherapy through the NHS. She later told me that he seemed exceptional in his desire to get well, which made her want to do everything she could to help him. Perhaps an even greater ally was another social worker named Tariq, who often bent the rules of Social Services to make sure that Terry would continue to receive his benefit and disability payments, in spite of the increasingly stringent requirements imposed by the government's austerity policy. Like Carol, he had been touched by Terry's plight, and felt compelled to do what he could to help him.

None of their acts of kindness could rescue Terry from his psychological condition. But they did provide him with vital lines of support without which his hope for improvement might have been entirely crushed.

It was somewhat disappointing then to learn how discouraged Terry became when he tried to look for paid employment. It wasn't that prospective employers had rejected him; it was that he couldn't overcome his anxiety about facing possible rejection in applying for a job. Just as he had loitered outside my consulting room when he was anxious about seeing me, he couldn't overcome his anxiety and enter the offices of potential employers to apply for work. With his mental health history, he felt sure no one would consider hiring him. His inability to surmount his fear and make an application sent him into a familiar spiral of shame and self-recrimination. Fortunately, Terry did eventually find work, though his position was unpaid. He got a volunteer job for a charity and also participated in a community gardening scheme which was established for people with mental health issues. Although he was disappointed that neither of these were what he regarded as a 'real job', he was conscientious in carrying out his responsibilities and he found a real benefit in working regularly and cooperatively with others. His supervisors and co-workers also appreciated his hard work and his helpfulness, just as he valued the camaraderie he found by working with others. Thanks to Tariq, his worries with the DSS ceased and he was no longer plagued by fears of being made homeless. These improvements in his living situation made a great difference to him, as he gratefully acknowledged to everyone who had given him assistance. Still, his sense of self continued to be defined by the loss of his family, a point that was made clear to him every time he went home to his empty flat. It had been more than twenty years since he lost his family, and he felt there was no reason to believe that this situation would ever change. Even so, he felt better about himself than he ever had after the death of his father.

*****

Whenever I look back at working with Terry, I take a measure of satisfaction in knowing he benefited from my support, though I regret that I couldn't help more. I also often found myself wishing that he could have found a therapeutic community to provide for both his psychic and social needs. His previous experiences of being sectioned, though clearly necessary for him at those times, could hardly meet his deeper need for self-integration. I was thinking of something along the lines of an asylum as R.D. Laing conceived the idea.

Laing's idea was to provide a supportive, nurturing community in which people could find their way through their internal conflicts to experience themselves with a renewed sense of self. He actually set up such a community in Kingsley Hall, a therapeutic household in the East End of London. Unfortunately, largely because of mismanagement, it lasted only a few years, though there are still a few therapeutic communities in Britain that are dedicated to providing similar support. But all of these communities were too distant from Terry's home for him to consider staying in any of them. I found this regrettable, as I believed that he might have benefited greatly by living in such a community.

As a therapist, I still regard the best work as that which leads a client to find resolution for a problem by achieving deeper self-insight, thereby finding both cause and remedy for what disturbs him. Yet, important as self-insight is, what matters at least as much is his ability to see how others experience him. In fact, self-insight doesn't come from introspection alone; it must also be achieved by deepening one's understanding of others. The insights that the client makes in psychotherapy can certainly help him do this, but the more important place for reaching a better understanding of others is in his actual everyday world, in his relationships with others. By this measure, Terry had certainly come a long way. Yet, I knew he was always likely to remain dependent on the kindness of others, as well as on the grudging charity of the state. I also believed that Terry would never be entirely free of the effects from the traumas he had suffered.

When I last saw Terry, he gave me a drawing of his, along with a poem he had written to express his appreciation for my help. But he had had enough of therapy, he said, and he wanted to stand on his own two feet without having to come talk to me. Knowing that his improvement was real, if somewhat fragile, I respected his decision. But even as I shook his hand and wished him well, I regretted his decision to leave and wished I could have done more for him. In truth, the skills of listening and analysing that all therapists must rely on, can do only so much. The shift towards healing and self-integration, which are the great desiderata of psychotherapy, also depends on other, sometimes mysterious factors that lie outside the therapist's ability to account for them. Chance and unforeseen circumstances – things beyond the purview of therapy – can either advance or impede the client's attempts to find deeper self-awareness and achieve greater self-reliance. In spite of the best efforts of both therapist and client, there can never be guaranteed outcomes in therapy. Yet, beneficial change can happen even in unexpected circumstances, and one of the skills that a therapist should cultivate is to recognise opportunities for positive change whenever they happen to arise. The key thing is to remain alert and open to the possibility of positive change even in times of doubt and uncertainty.

The feeling of being blessed by the universe that Terry experienced when he looked out at the night sky over the Atlantic with his father never occurred to him again. After all his misfortunes, he might have been justified in thinking the universe was actually capricious and heartless. But metaphysical speculation of any sort is of little use for therapy and I wouldn't encourage any of my clients to indulge in it. Yet, sometimes only a belief in some benevolent higher power seems to enable people to endure their lives of terrible suffering. A universe ordered with cold indifference to suffering, however in keeping with modern sensibilities, may only deepen a vulnerable person's despair, whereas believing in a benevolent spiritual power may at least offer some hope and consolation. But true benevolence doesn't come from the majesty of a universe whose design we can never comprehend. It comes from the compassion of one person recognising and working to ease another person's suffering. And though psychotherapy should aspire to do more than dispense acts of kindness, sometimes it is all that therapy can do. I never saw or heard from Terry again. But I still believe that therapy was one of the things that managed to help him.

A Question of Love

It's easy to see why someone like George would turn to psychotherapy in a time of grief, as therapy allows a bereaved person to reflect on the loss of a beloved partner beyond the usual rituals of mourning. But helping people deal with grief is only one concern of therapy, and there are countless other reasons for people to seek therapeutic help. Certainly, depressions like Suzy suffered, and childhood traumas like Terry experienced, are also common reasons. But psychological misery can arise from any number of causes, and while they may all share certain features in common, on close inspection every case turns out to be unique. As a therapist, then, I avoid making a generalised, medical sounding diagnosis precisely because it discourages the client from developing the individual self-awareness that therapy depends on. Moreover, I don't believe that a purely objective medical diagnosis for psychological conditions is actually possible. Although I believe identifiable patterns of mental suffering are a reality beyond dispute, the idea that there are discrete disease entities that can account for them has little, if any, merit in my view.

Nevertheless, having some theoretical understanding of what people typically experience when they are depressed, anxious or deeply confused, is a resource that no therapist can do without. But this mostly applies at an early stage of therapy. Once the therapist reaches a working understanding of the client, helping her look beyond the symptoms of her particular condition to find the true, if unacknowledged, intentions that holds her condition in place, becomes the essential task of therapy.

This almost always involves recalling painful experiences from the past, as well as looking at difficulties and frustrations in the present. And what is often discovered is that at the heart of those frustrations there is a terrible privation that can be both mysterious and obvious at the same time – the lack of love in the life of the client. What, then, can therapy do about such a privation?

The idea that getting love is the answer for all the pains and frustrations to which the self is subject is practically a cliché, and every therapist should regard it with deep suspicion. Unfortunately, not all therapists do, and many err seriously by identifying too strongly with their clients' desire for love, and imposing their narrative predilections into the living story of their clients. A recently divorced therapist, for example, might advise her client to be more distrustful of her marriage partner than the reality of the case warrants. This may be done more or less innocently, but it is almost always done blindly, and can only work against the client's need to develop self-insight. Perhaps even worse are therapists who explicitly advertise themselves as love doctors, offering wisdom and advice for obtaining love and sex. There are certainly good, ethical therapists who deal responsibly with issues relating to sex and relationships. Unfortunately, there are also many others who are only too willing to exploit the insecurity of their clients by selling success in love as a simple matter of gratifying desire.

A brilliant psychologist, the late David Smail, used to argue that a key strategy of the advertising industry is to present love as a scarce commodity by convincing people that only the wealthy, famous, intelligent or beautiful are worthy of it. And to the extent that therapists leave such beliefs unchallenged, they collaborate with consumerism in convincing people that they're not good enough as they are. Though Smail was clearly right about that, feeling deprived of love is nothing new or modern. The complaint of the world has always been that there is not enough love to go around. The problem that therapists will always face is the absence of love in the lives of our clients. "Why doesn't love happen to me?" or, even more poignantly, "why didn't love happen in my childhood, when I needed it the most?" are questions that come up regularly in therapy. Some cases are particularly heart wrenching.

Julie was an only child whose parents divorced when she was five, without anyone explaining the split to her. One day her father simply moved out of her house and her mother was forced to take a job at a local supermarket. While her mother worked, Julie spent a great deal of time at home alone watching television. Although her dad used to visit once a fortnight, he never mentioned that he had married again or that his second wife had given birth to another daughter. One day when she was ten, a five-year-old girl got out of the car with her dad, who said that this beautiful little girl was actually her little sister. Julie stared at the little girl in disbelief and as she watched her half-sister playing contentedly with dolls that she had outgrown, she couldn't quite shake off the feeling that this was all a very strange, rather terrible dream. The feeling intensified as she watched the little girl get back in the car to go back home with her dad – to go to their home, leaving Julie alone with her uncommunicative mum. She began to feel angry at her dad and wrote him a letter which said if he wouldn't see her more often then she didn't want to see him at all.

He wrote back and said fine, Julie, you won't see me at all, then – and he kept his word. Her father's letter, and his subsequent absence from her life, left Julie with a hollow feeling which seemed to engulf her. She felt as if all her feelings had been sucked out of her, leaving her with a sense of being strangely disembodied. A single mother on benefit now, she has had a succession of relationships with men who invariably mistreat her before leaving in a cold fury. She always feels hollowed out afterwards, just like she felt when her dad left her. Then she gets together with another man who mistreats her before leaving her, making her feel empty... and so on.

*****

Everyone agreed that there was no trusting Conor. A small, weedy boy of sixteen, he seemed all too eager to please and annoyingly desperate to make friends. Even worse, Conor was a petty thief who had a habit of stealing objects that were practically worthless in themselves, but important to the people who owned them.

Rulers, pens and other small items all had a way of winding up in his possession, though he would always deny that he had taken them. I found them, he would say, as if the items had simply dropped into his hands by accident. No one believed his ridiculous excuses so his reputation as a thief was fatally coupled with his reputation for being a liar. Eventually, he was caught in the act of stealing a pocket calculator, and some of the harder lads who had always hated him anyway, decided they had had enough. They would teach him a lesson that he would never forget. Conor sensed that he was in danger and was agile enough to evade his attackers for a time. But eventually he was cornered in a secluded place and beaten savagely.

Conor didn't show up to school for a week after his beating and people thought perhaps he would never come back. But he returned later as if nothing had happened. In fact, a beating wasn't unusual for Conor. His father used to beat him regularly, usually for small mistakes, but sometimes for no other reason than his mere physical presence. The actual, underlying reason was that Conor wasn't his biological son, but was the offspring of a night of casual sex between Conor's constantly drunken mother and a man she had barely known and could not have remembered if she tried. After giving birth to Conor, his mum was usually too drunk to deal with him so his nominal father looked after his needs, though in a way that was entirely bereft of affection. "Useless bastard", his dad always used to say after a beating.

*****

For psychotherapists, there would be nothing particularly unusual about these two cases. The difficulty would be to see past the massive damage inflicted on the victims to find emotional possibility amidst the ruins of their childhood experiences. Indeed, these two stories offer textbook examples of childhood abuse, so much so that a therapist would need to be careful not to suppose that he knows more about the victims' suffering than they do. Nevertheless, it would be easy for a therapist to identify what the clients clearly unable to see: a pattern of misery which had originated in childhood keeps repeating itself through actions that the victims initiate, yet fail to understand. When, for example, Julie goes into yet another abusive relationship, it is both new and strangely familiar to her; though seen objectively its novelty would seem to depend on her wilful blindness. And when Conor antagonises those whose approval he craves, the futility of his behaviour is exceeded only by his lack of self-insight. Like everybody else, they too, want love and approval. But in their desperation for love and acceptance, it seems as if Julie and Conor set out to demonstrate that they do not actually deserve it.

Smail argues that love is inherently dangerous because people will surrender almost anything to get it, and in the capitalist dispensation, love functions as a virtually unattainable prize of a cut-throat competition for self-validation. In any such competition, people like Julie and Conor would enter the contest destined to lose. For it is a game they hardly know how to play and whose unspoken rules seem designed to trip them up. Of course, it can be objected that true love is nothing like this, and that true love is precisely what they need. But this raises the almost impossible question: what is true love, as distinct from the counterfeits people confuse it for?

The acclaimed psychotherapist and writer, Irving Yalom, describes himself as love's executioner, whose duty as a therapist is to destroy the illusions on which love thrives. I admire Yalom and largely agree with him. Yet, I believe a therapist must proceed cautiously in annihilating the illusions of love as those illusions may offer valuable insights into the experience of the client. Julie, for instance, always feels hesitant before going into another abusive relationship. Her lack of self-insight indicates the intensity of her emotional needs, and the intensity of her needs thwarts the development of her self-insight. All of this might be dismissed as little more than the rat run of a pathological process. Yet Julie's moment of hesitation may hold the key to the self-insight that would prevent her from going into yet another disastrous relationship. To be sure, the key to her hesitation will be hard to find, and her search will likely evoke much anxiety. But it is by expressing her anxiety and giving voice to her blind longing for love that Julie may discover why her relationships always replicate the pattern of failed love that she first experienced with her father. This, however, may only tell her why her desire never becomes realised as love, and may offer little clue as to how love might actually be found.

For a Buddhist therapist, dealing with a client's desire for love seldom accords with the precepts of the Buddhadharma. Moreover, Buddhism remains largely silent about the benefits of romantic love, though it does provide an abundance of wisdom for the cultivation of kindness and compassion, virtues which may be regarded as selfless forms of love. Offering little support for romance, these virtues aim only to increase a person's capacity for selfless, caring interactions with others. Buddhism frowns on romantic love largely because it regards any sort of passionate attachment as a disguised form of misery. The second Noble Truth of Buddhism even states explicitly that craving is the primary source of all suffering, and Buddhist teaching goes on to warn that craving can be particularly dangerous when it presents itself as irresistible desire. But for someone like Julie, chasing desire doesn't promise the fulfilment of a craving so much as it represents rescue from the emotional privation from which she has always suffered. Desperate for love, she has only a vague notion of what the actual experience of love could be. Letting go of her desire for love is all but unthinkable. Though it is certainly a form of craving, it also represents one of the few hopes she has.

"Why can't I experience love?" is the burning question that takes many people into therapy, often with the hope that a therapist can provide an easy answer. That there are no easy answers – certainly none that a therapist can provide – is the place for therapy to begin. Gradually, as the therapeutic alliance develops, a deeper self-awareness may take root in the client, which may not only free her desire for love from its compulsive force and its self-alienating urgency, but may also make finding a loving relationship more likely. No longer an unattainable object of desire, love becomes a way of knowing oneself and wanting to know others. Therapy can be the place for the quest for such self-knowledge to begin. But it should never be the place where it ends.

Crooked Timber

When people turn to therapy, they often feel conflicted and bewildered by the emotional state they find themselves in. Sometimes they can trace the cause of their distress to particular incidents or living conditions, but often they're simply baffled by their feelings, and wonder what makes them feel so painfully confused. Their distress may even lead them to believe that if they were like other people they wouldn't be suffering as they do – a belief that must be rejected before real change can occur. The idea that imitating others can bring actual happiness is only likely to increase their frustrations, and will never solve their problems. Being different from other people isn't their problem; it's their inability to deal with the painful situations they find themselves in. Moreover, it is only when they recognise their uniqueness as individuals that they can go on to find the resources to deal with the problems that afflict them. This may not make them normal as they conceive it, but it can bring the self-acceptance that will enable them to lead richer and more fulfilled lives.

When I first met a client called Simon I was reminded of Immanuel Kant's famous epigram: "Out of the crooked timber of humanity, no straight thing can be made." Though Simon was a young man in his late twenties, he still retained the shambling awkwardness that affects many boys throughout their adolescence. His somewhat diffident, dishevelled appearance was made more pronounced by his initial reluctance to make eye contact with me, though his shyness did allow me to look more closely at his appearance. Simon's socks didn't match; his trousers were a bit too short; and there was a grease spot halfway down his rumpled shirt. Almost inevitably, his hair was in disarray, which suggested that he might have suffered a moment of confusion before the mirror that morning. Looking artfully dishevelled can be rather fashionable these days, but Simon was simply a bit of a mess, not just in his presentation, but in his personal life, too. He complained that he was suffering from mild, chronic depression, though he sometimes suffered from moments of acute anxiety as well. But there was little mystery as to the source of his problem, he thought. At almost thirty years of age, Simon was still a virgin and believed that his lack of sexual experience was a sure sign that there must be something terribly defective with him. It was not that he regarded his virginity as a sign of mental illness; it just seemed a strong indication that there was something wrong with his entire way of being. After all, nobody else he knew seemed to be deprived of sexual experience as he was. He just wanted what everybody else had. He wanted to be normal.

I confess I had to resist a strong temptation to give Simon some fatherly advice. I would have begun by suggesting that he should pay more attention to his appearance, if only for him to become aware of how his shambolic self-presentation made him appear to others. I might have also counselled him to straighten his back, and while he was at it, to look me in the eye when he was speaking to me. "Show a bit of confidence, boy, and maybe the girls will begin to find you a bit more attractive", would have been the gist of my advice. Though the advice would have been meant to help him, it would have been patronising in every sense of the word, and I knew it would accomplish nothing. Moreover, Simon was not a boy, even if he appeared to be stuck in a particularly painful phase of adolescence. What I needed to learn is why he found himself so estranged from the normal life that he seemed to think would be forever outside of his reach. I began by asking him to tell me about his past.

There was nothing particularly unusual about Simon's upbringing. He was born in a middle-sized town in Kent to a family of modest means. His father was employed as an engineer for an electrical appliance firm, and his mother worked as a nurse. He had two older sisters who were now married with small children and were following much the same path in life that their parents had travelled. A capable student, Simon attended a grammar school where he was particularly strong in science and maths. Later, he studied computer science at a London university where he attained a solid 2:1 degree, which put him in a favourable position to land a decent paying job upon graduating. The one shadow in this otherwise satisfying picture was that all through his secondary school years Simon had difficulty making friends. He was eager to do so but he lacked the gift of sociability that everyone else seemed to possess naturally.

Even worse, he also had to put up with a considerable amount of derision, usually by serving as the butt of jokes. He was quick to forgive these offences, however, and sometimes he even tried to embrace the role of fool in the vain hope of winning approval from his antagonists. Unfortunately, his gambit only increased the contempt they felt for him, and after a time he learned to fade into the background whenever he felt people were about to become hostile. Eventually, he accepted his place on the fringe of the social life to which others seemed to enjoy such easy access.

That Simon had always been among the first to be excluded socially by his peers when he was in secondary school was hardly surprising. Adolescence, at least in most advanced capitalist societies, can be a time of ruthless competition for popularity and prestige based on attractiveness and social savoir faire. Although he was not notably unattractive as a teenager, his social clumsiness, combined with his helpless eagerness to please others, doomed him to be an outcast. Yet, for all of his social awkwardness and the uncertainty he felt about dealing with people as an adolescent, the longer he dealt with me the more impressed I was by how remarkably considerate, even sensitive he could be. In such simple things as how he made way for me as we went into my consulting room, or how he listened politely when I was speaking, Simon's courtesy seemed an indelible feature of his personality. What he conveyed in these simple gestures was a capacity for care, a rare, if somewhat undervalued characteristic these days. Still, consideration for others usually counts as an asset in forming relationships of all kinds, including romantic ones. So I was forced to wonder why his considerateness seemed to bring so little advantage in his social life.

It turned out that after secondary school Simon was in fact regarded as a fairly likeable fellow by almost everyone who knew him. But he disregarded any suggestion of his likeability. He felt more tolerated than liked and believed that no one felt any real affection for him. There was, he thought, good reason for their lack of interest, as well. No doubt his self-perception had its origins in his experience at secondary school, but he still believed that there was something defective in himself and he would never be quite acceptable to others. And as for finding romance, that seemed entirely beyond him.

Dislodging a deeply held belief is never easy, but if the belief is foundational to someone's self-understanding, then uprooting it may appear virtually impossible. Still, there is some mystery as to why some people become so strongly attached to the negative identities that have been imposed on them. It is as if they have become defined by the attributions others have made about them, and those self-definitions come to seem natural, even if they remain constant sources of stress. The scorn that victims of ostracisation may have experienced in the past becomes a kind of inner truth, even when other, later experiences have presented more favourable ways of regarding themselves. This is particularly true for infants and small children. The deprivation of love and respect in early childhood can follow unloved children like a curse throughout their lives. But even though Simon felt his family was caring if not particularly demonstrative, the security of his childhood gave him few clues for dealing with others later in life.

In truth, though self-discovery does begin in infancy and early childhood, it does not, and cannot, end there. Throughout our lives we discover, or rather rediscover, who we are in our interactions with others. And though childhood is a particularly tender and formative stage of personal development, adolescence is also fraught with difficulties of its own. My question to Simon was about why he was unable to see himself in a more positive light after secondary school, when he was no longer a victim of disapproval by his peers and was regarded more favourably by his colleagues. But my question puzzled him, and he seemed astonished by the suggestion that he could have experienced himself in any other way. Though he conceded that people tended to be friendlier to him as he became older, he supposed that was because people became more polite with age, not because he had become worthier of affection. His observation surprised me and led me to ask if he thought he still deserved the disrespect he once suffered. He chuckled and said no, but he felt no more worthy of respect, either. Quite simply, he felt there was no reason why anyone should regard him in a favourable light.

Given his experience of adolescence, it was easy to see why Simon was given to depression, but his anxiety was somewhat more difficult to understand. For he tended to suffer panic not when he felt lonely in the company of other people, but when he was alone and not under any particular stress. He first experienced a panic attack when he had been working long hours on a project that often required him to stay late in his office. He remembered coming home late one night and drinking a beer before collapsing onto his bed without even undressing. He woke up at 3:00 in the morning, disturbed by a dream that he couldn't quite remember. But he felt very afraid, and perhaps even worse, he felt acutely alone in his fear. He attributed his anxiety to the heavy stress of work and a lack of sleep, and it did seem that these actually were significant factors in causing his panic. Wisely then, he made a point of preparing himself properly for sleep and avoiding late hours at work, and these measures did help make him calmer. Yet, anxiety continued to haunt him and there were times when he would feel overwhelmed, usually when he was alone at home. It was difficult for him to identify exactly what triggered these attacks. They usually occurred after he had been absorbed in some ordinary activity such as tidying his house or playing a computer game. But then, just when his attention shifted away from whatever he was doing, he would suddenly be stricken by pervasive anxiety. "Over nothing", he said, still mystified as to the source of his sudden, inexplicable distress. But it wasn't really nothing that caused his panic; it was, rather, nothing he could find.

It is anxiety, not love, that makes the world go around, but the fear of not finding love is among the greatest sources of anxiety that anyone can experience. Although Simon believed that his virginity was at the root of his distress, I thought it more likely that shame was the true cause of his anxiety. He was frank in admitting the absence of a sexual partner made him turn to online pornography for sexual release and that he used to binge on porn periodically until he became consumed by self-disgust, only to resume his habit later. But he claimed to find nothing wrong, at least morally, with either masturbation or pornography, as he felt both were natural ways of relieving his sexual craving. Still, he couldn't quite shake the feeling that indulging in them reinforced his sense of sexual inadequacy. Just a stupid wanker, he described himself. No wonder women didn't find him attractive, he thought. But I suspected that he still might have formed erotic attachments to particular women that may have contributed to his anxiety. My hunch proved correct, as he admitted that he had always regarded a succession of beautiful women with worshipful adoration. Generally, he didn't dare speak to the women he was attracted to, for he supposed that he was virtually non-existent in their eyes. So he was surprised when a work colleague, a bright, vivacious young woman named Sarah, actually seemed to regard him with some interest. She chatted freely, at times almost flirtatiously with him, and though it took him a while to permit himself the thought, he eventually began to believe, in his words, that "she was sort of attracted to me". Although he never seriously entertained the idea that he could be romantically linked with Sarah, the mere idea that someone he found so attractive would consider him appealing felt uplifting for him. But then his bubble burst.

His painful revelation came one evening when he joined a number of colleagues from his office for drinks at a pub. At first, the scene was quite merry, with laughter flowing as freely as the drinks. But then the mood gradually flattened, and levity gave way to something far less congenial. Although everybody was still laughing, the laughter had become sullen and mirthless. Simon made the mistake of trying to make a risqué joke – he couldn't quite remember exactly what he said, but it was some clumsy allusion to the size of his penis – and he knew he had made a mistake as soon as he spoke. No one laughed, and an uncomfortable silence instantly descended over the gathering. It was as if he had been discovered as the reason for what was turning into a dismal night out. He tried to apologise, but that only seemed to make things worse. But what was most disturbing to him was Sarah's reaction. When he turned to look at her she refused to meet his eyes and seemed faintly repelled by his presence. He sat in embarrassed silence before withdrawing as quietly as he could. Walking home that night he wept as he remembered what a fool he had been. The evening reminded him of his true identity – a hopeless clod, a dejected buffoon, a nobody. He would never make the mistake of overestimating himself again.

Simon and I spent a lot of time recalling his experience of that night at the pub. Even though his problem clearly did not originate in the incident, it did seem to confirm the truth of his self understanding, or rather, he believed it did. My view of the event was that perhaps it was not quite the catastrophe he thought it was. Although heavy drinking can certainly bring out embarrassing behaviour in people, relatively minor transgressions of judgement or taste may be forgotten, if not entirely forgiven, if alcohol was involved. My hunch gained credence when Simon said that when he returned to work on the following Monday nobody mentioned the embarrassing incident, and Sarah seemed her usual bright and effervescent self. I tried to suggest that perhaps he had exaggerated the effect of his faux pas. But he dismissed the idea. and felt he had learned a painful lesson. He was not about to risk further humiliation by pretending that his acquaintance with someone as attractive as Sarah was deeper than it actually was. Whatever the actual truth of the evening, we were not going to repair the damage by mulling over its details any further. More important, I thought, was for him to be able to reflect on his disappointment without allowing it to become self-defining.

Simon had one thing going for him which I believe is essential for the success of any therapeutic relationship. He was committed to therapy, even when it seemed to be going nowhere. His life had always had a regularity about it, sometimes to the point of monotony, and he had always found some security in adhering to an established routine. Fitting in an hour for therapy each week soon became a welcome break for him. Our task, however, was not to let therapy become merely routine or a way of spending an hour talking idly about familiar things. Keeping wonder alive about commonplace or routine events is how therapy enables clients to find fresh possibilities for themselves. It makes change possible by reflecting on, and questioning, the pattern of day-to-day events that sustains the client's sense of self. This requires patience, however, sometimes more from the therapist than the client. For the wonder that the therapist brings to the client's description of his ordinary, day-to-day activities can serve as a stimulus to the client's sense of wonder, encouraging him to see beneath his own stated intentions and beliefs about his life to discover what really drives his actions. Unfortunately, it often seems that many clients would rather not see things in a new light and prefer to cling to unthinking routine as a form of security.

Every week, I would encourage Simon to look at his day-to-day affairs from a fresh perspective and try to get him to remove the blinkers of his mental habits. At times he seemed to rise to the opportunity for meaningful self-reflection, but mostly he was unable to see beyond his habitual ways of thinking and feeling. There were some seemingly minor changes, evidenced by his ease of communication and his dress sense (which no longer seemed as hopelessly sloppy as it first did), but I still wondered if we were getting anywhere. The irony, of course, is that having a fixed goal is something I try to avoid as a therapist. Although therapy should attempt to help the client find better possibilities, a therapist should keep an open mind about how the client will make these discoveries. He should also remember that the client's discoveries do not always emerge from the therapeutic encounter, but may arise in the course of everyday living. Therapy may act as a positive influence, but sometimes something more like fate seems to intervene.

I was on the verge of losing hope that Simon would ever find enough insight to free himself of his tendency to depression and anxiety. But a breakthrough came unexpectedly when he returned to his hometown for a visit one weekend and met a woman named Erin, a friend of one of his sisters. It seemed Erin may have been in a rather vulnerable position herself as she had recently gone through a divorce. But when she encountered Simon she seemed unaccountably delighted to see him. At first it was strange, he said, for he had only a vague memory of her before he left home for university, and never considered her in any sort of romantic light. But when he realised that she was attracted to him and wanted to go to bed with him, he didn't hesitate to act on the opportunity. Their affair was brief, intense, and mutually enjoyable, but she let him know that it could be nothing more than a fling. Even so, their lovemaking was tender and passionate, and exceeded anything he had ever imagined in his lonely masturbatory fantasies. In meeting her desire with his, Simon experienced a deep mutuality of feeling, something that he might have been tempted to call love except that he knew she didn't want him to say the word. I was astonished, and though I didn't express my surprise openly, it must have been revealed in my rather oafish question to him.

"What did she see in you?"

"She said she knew I would be caring", he said with disarming candour. And then, he added: "I was, too".

I admit I was stunned into silence by his innocent reply.

It was not immediately apparent to me that Simon's affair would have any lasting impact on him. After all, one brief affair, no matter how enjoyable, can hardly be an indicator of lasting wellbeing. Yet, in losing his virginity he felt he had crossed a threshold. I also found it encouraging that his initiation into sex with a partner also gave him a tender experience of intimacy and trust. But what he found most beneficial was that he realised that he was not an outcast or a misfit, but only someone whose first experience of sex with a partner had come later than most people's. At last, he felt normal! For my part, I was pleased that Simon no longer felt stigmatised by his late virginity, but I had hoped that he would feel more than merely normal. I had wished that in feeling fully human, he would also have felt uniquely himself.

But the thought never occurred to him, which made me realise that I was projecting my hopes on to him. Still, he seemed satisfied by the way things had turned out, and that, I suppose, was good enough.

It wasn't too long after his affair that Simon quit seeing me and took a job in Dubai. I had a hunch that we were close to terminating after his affair with Erin, as his mood had brightened considerably, and his anxiety attacks had vanished, as well. He also seemed far more at ease with me, yet at the same time, less dependent on our weekly appointments. I felt reasonably confident that he was going to be alright once he settled in Dubai, but after our last appointment I never heard from him again. Because Simon never presented symptoms of a debilitating mental illness and had a brighter outlook upon ending therapy, it seemed safe to assume that he was going to be okay. But the question of how someone will go on to live after therapy is rather different from the question of his remaining free of mental illness. The notions of mental illness and mental health, indispensable though they may be, tell us only so much about the actual life experience of a person, or how that person experiences himself in pursuit of the things that matter to him. Once I lost contact with Simon, I was in no position to know about him. But I still wonder: did he like his new job? Did he make new friends? And did he ever find another romantic partner? Almost anything could have happened. But I never found out.

Most of all, I wonder how psychotherapy helped Simon. He claimed it did, and I tend to agree, but I still wonder how. After all, therapy didn't seem to produce any deep self-insights for him. It's also quite possible that he could have resolved his problems without my help. He still could have lost his virginity, freeing him to go on to live a more or less satisfactory life, and becoming less depressed and less prone to anxiety. But perhaps by offering Simon the opportunity for self-reflection in conditions of deep trust, therapy helped make intimacy with Erin possible. If therapy failed to produce any deep self-insights for him, it still suggested that it was possible for him to encounter another person with openness and trust, and perhaps even love. This was hardly medicine, let alone any sort of objective science. But psychotherapy reached him as a human being in a way that a more medical approach never could. Moreover, therapy seemed to work for Simon in a way that was relevant to his interests and needs, not the ones I was tempted to impose on him. Though my influence was hardly neutral, my hopes for him didn't interfere with the aim he began with, either. He wanted to feel normal. By the time he ended therapy with me, he did. But I don't think therapy really straightened him out. It just made his crookedness more acceptable to him.

In Dreams Begin Responsibilities

"The interpretation of dreams is the royal road to a knowledge of
the unconscious activities of the mind."

Sigmund Freud, *The Interpretation of Dreams*

It is now well over a century since the publication of Freud's
revolutionary *The Interpretation of Dreams*, a book that claimed to
reveal the function of unconscious processes by offering a radically new
approach to dream interpretation. The enigmatic nature of dreams had
always demanded specialists to interpret them and find the eerie
meaning that seemed to emerge from their apparently nonsensical
contents. But Freud was original by insisting that his new medical
science of psychoanalysis was uniquely equipped to make scientific
sense of the dream lives of his patients. The psychoanalytic conception
of unconscious processes, which Freud claimed was essential for
understanding human nature and experience, depended a great deal on
the knowledge that he had acquired from his research into dreams. Yet
his approach to dream interpretation was based on a fairly simple
axiom: dreams express the unfulfilled wishes of the dreamer, and are
disguised by a variety of unconscious stratagems that aim to preserve
the dreamer's psychic equilibrium. Although critics of psychoanalysis
have always rejected this sweeping, categorical assertion, Freud
adamantly maintained that his theory of dreams was the key to
unlocking the secrets of the unconscious. Dream interpretation not
only provided a vital therapeutic technique for practising
psychoanalysis, he argued; it also confirmed his theoretical concepts by
revealing the inner life of the dreamer.

Over the century since Freud first advanced his ideas about dreams, there has been a remarkable decline in interest in dream interpretation among psychotherapists of other schools. Old school psychoanalysts of both the Freudian and Jungian variety are still trained in dream interpretation, but dreamwork has never featured importantly in most other approaches. And as for psychiatry, it has turned away almost entirely from exploring the subjective experiences of its patients in favour of a biological understanding of their complaints. One consequence of this neglect is that most psychiatrists nowadays tend to dismiss dreams as little more than meaningless phenomenological fluff. In my own training, an unorthodox, but innovative blend of Buddhism and Rogerian psychology, dreams hardly figured in the teaching at all. Fortunately, in undergoing therapy for my training, I chose a Jungian analyst who made my dream life a focus of our work together. Every night I recorded my dreams and then emailed them to my analyst, who kept them on file.

Sometimes we would examine a dream closely, but at other times we wouldn't discuss my dreams at all. Even so, having my dreams recorded by me, and read by him, brought the oneiric dimension of my experience into our interactions, even when we didn't actually examine any dream material. Through my emails, we were both aware that my dreams had entered the consulting room before I did. And by working with my dreams on a daily basis, I came to realise that in some uncanny way my dreams preceded all my waking experiences. In therapy, I began to appreciate what Delmore Schwartz must have meant by the title of his best known story: in dreams begin responsibilities.

For all of the psychological treasures that dreams are supposed to hold, working with them does require effort. Most dreaming escapes conscious recall, and even those dreams that can be remembered usually require some effort of recollection. The need to make an effort points to the inherent difficulty of making sense of dreams. Details that are fuzzy or insensible are easily forgotten, and the same censoring mentality that surveils all the dreamer's conscious acts may exert a repressive influence on the recollection of her dreams, as well. Though many therapists might agree with psychoanalysis that dreams are the royal road to the unconscious, they may still doubt that the road leads to anywhere of importance. In my work, however, I have found that dreams reward examination by opening up a domain of unconscious fantasy that acts as a potent force in waking life, even though this realm is mostly hidden and unseen. Indeed, fantasy gains in potency the more unseen and less conscious it is. By exploring dreams, therapy can reveal the hidden fantasies of clients unconstrained by outer realities, or the inhibitions of conscience. Ideally, dreamwork will help the client develop a deeper awareness of the unconscious processes that give rise to her sense of self.

The difficulty for many people is that their dreams often seem too vague or meaningless to bother with. Other people sometimes find their dreams so shameful that they actively try to ignore them. Freud regarded both reactions as forms of resistance, but I tend to see these attitudes as natural reluctance to find sense or meaning in the confusion and obscurity of dreams. But by disarming the client of the fear that as a therapist I might have more understanding of her dreams than she does, I can usually ease her anxieties about exploring them. I even have a simple rule for working with the dreams of my clients: the dreamer's feelings about her dreams have priority over any interpretation I might make. I can still share my ideas about the significance of a dream, but my ideas should never overrule the dreamer's feelings. Dream work in this approach is less about analysing the content of dreams than it is about helping the client develop an emotional connection to her dream life and finding a window into her unconscious processes. Though interpretation still has a place in this approach, it is based on the premise that a dream becomes meaningful to the extent that it becomes an object of personal reflection.

Remembering dreams may be difficult at first, but with practice recall can usually be improved. Still, sometimes effective recall amounts to nothing more than catching fragmentary images and extrapolating the feeling tone from them. Remembering a dream in this way is less concerned with preserving its content fully than it is with remaining alert to its affective influence. In fact, it is the feeling tone of a dream that often proves to be most useful for remembering its details, though it is also essential for revealing its emotional importance. The important thing, I believe, is to keep the dream alive as a glowing ember of remembrance. Recording a dream immediately upon waking is perhaps the best way of remembering it, though my preferred method is to brew a cup of coffee before writing it down on my laptop. I find the brief period before the cobwebs of slumber have entirely dissipated gives me time to recall the dream in depth. There is no way of knowing if my method makes recollection of the dream any more, or less, accurate than other methods of recall, but it does help me to preserve the mood of the dream as I make my transition to daytime consciousness. It is also a good way to find the deeper layers of meaning in a dream, and perhaps even find the roots of unconscious fantasy, which the dream can present in revealing ways.

I once dealt with a man who dreamt of a girlfriend he had lost, years after they had broken up. In his dream, his girlfriend was now married to someone he didn't recognise, but who seemed "bright, relaxed, a really attractive guy". Out of their sight, my client listened in anguish as his girlfriend was speaking to her dream husband about how unhappy she had been in her relationship with the dreamer. She expressed regret that she had had anything to do with him at all. My client woke up profoundly saddened over a loss that he had all but forgotten. At first, he believed that the dream must have meant that he still missed a once cherished lover. And though this might have been true enough at some level, a more significant truth lay beneath it. He found it by focussing on his feeling of sadness and reflecting on the figure of her husband, recognising him as someone who was truly capable of love in painful contrast to his own manifest failings as a lover. His girlfriend's dream husband was the man he had not been and felt he never could be. And the sadness that found expression in this dream turned out to be a key element of the chronic depression that he had suffered for most of his adult life.

Not all dreams represent things with such apt symbolism, and sometimes they seem to express nothing meaningful at all. Freud claimed that there was an inverse relation between how meaningless a dream seems and its actual significance. The 'crazier' the dream the more meaningful it is, he argued. His claim gave psychoanalysts broad licence for interpretation and disposed their patients to defer to the expert opinion of the analyst. But there is little hard evidence for his claim. Even so, it is the phenomenology, or experience, of dreaming that has always attracted the greater interest of psychotherapists. And because dreams often present themselves as obscure riddles, it seems to require something akin to a literary skill to decode their meaning. But occasionally a dream can be as factual as a news report.

A client of mine who was having a problem with his marriage came in one day with an ashen look on his face because of a recent dream his wife had had. On the very night he was away on a business trip and having a liaison with another woman behind her back, she had a vivid dream of his adulterous encounter. "How could you?", his wife shouted at him over the phone the following morning. The apparent clairvoyance of her dream flabbergasted him, but I was just as mystified as he was. Sometimes, it seems, a dream will know more than the dreamer should be able to know. But it is rare for the meaning to be as transparent as the dream of my client's wife.

Any dream that holds great emotional force can seem to contain an important message for the dreamer, even though the message might be obscure or unwelcome. Nightmares fall into this category, and because of the terror they provoke, they must be treated with a great deal of sensitivity. They often occur after some trauma, and the terror people suffer seems to be the result of replaying the more frightening features of the traumatic event in a dream.

Victims of physical violence or sexual assault are particularly susceptible to nightmares, but any event which poses a threat to the dreamer's sense of self can cause one. A loss of a relationship or job often triggers one, as can the death of someone close to the dreamer. But people can suffer nightmares even from a virtual trauma or loss. My sister Barbara used to suffer periodic nightmares throughout her childhood after watching the 1939 film version of *The Wizard of Oz* on television, and conceiving a special dread for the Wicked Witch of the West. It was only as an adult, after reading the obituary of Margaret Hamilton, the actress who played the role so convincingly, that Barbara had her last nightmare of the terrible witch who had haunted her childhood dreams. Of course, it may have been that her dreams about the Wicked Witch were provoked by things which made her feel as vulnerable as Dorothy. But what held her captive to her childhood terror were the dreams that expressed it. She didn't have those dreams; those dreams had her. But then, this is true of almost everybody's dreams. Our dreams possess us and hold us in their thrall, until we wake up and their spell is broken. But how then do we make sense of them?

Contrary to what Freud seemed to believe, dream interpretation is not an exact science, and given the uniquely personal references within a dream to the life of the dreamer, it is difficult to see how it could be. Moreover, the science of dreaming has advanced greatly since Freud's time and much more is known about it now, particularly as a biological phenomenon, than he could have ever known. We now know, for example, that much of the function of dreaming is for pruning memory of all the trivial impressions that a person gathers from conscious experience in the course of a day. Laboratory research also suggests that dreaming attempts to maintain the emotional equilibrium of the dreamer, particularly after a traumatic event. Freud's views still enjoy wide respect, perhaps, in part, because he had the first word in the modern, psychological interpretation of dreams. But the idea that a dream must express the unfulfilled wishes of the dreamer is no longer generally accepted, even though many dreams appear to do just that.

Olivia, a barrister specialising in international law, had a recurring dream that featured a stereotypical macho man whom she dubbed Mr Wrong. Mr Wrong was quite unlike the man she was actually seeing. Her dream lover was handsome, virile and – rather embarrassingly for her – utterly sexist in his treatment of her. Roger, the man that she was actually seeing, was a shy introvert who made cautious overtures for sex, if he dared to make them at all. Her erotic dreams made her ashamed, for she hated the type of man who dominated her sleep – but only in her waking states. In her dreams, her submission to him was thrilling, in part, she knew, because her pleasure overruled her expressed values and beliefs. But the idea that her dreams revealed that she might not be the principled feminist she considered herself to be was still rather shameful for her. If there was ever a client who seemed to prove Freud's dictum about dreams as the fulfilment of forbidden wishes, it was Olivia. Yet it would have been a mistake to regard her unwanted erotic dreams as entirely indicative of her actual character. Olivia was a complex and principled person with diverse interests who entered therapy in order to come to terms with this apparent conflict within her character. But if she wasn't the hypocrite that she feared she was, why did she have such disturbing, shameful dreams? This was best answered by tracing the relevance of her dreams to her waking life.

Olivia's dream life was actually quite rich and varied, with dreams that could be curious, puzzling or faintly ominous, depending on the mood she found herself in. They were usually set in locations familiar to her, such as her home or place of work. Occasionally, they harked back to earlier times or places in her life, such as the house where she spent her childhood, or the city where she attended university. The people who appeared in her dreams were often familiar figures from her life: family, friends and work colleagues appeared along with other people she didn't recognise at all. But no one in her dreams disturbed her quite so much as Mr Wrong. In fact, there was no one in her life who really resembled him, and if he was like anyone, it might have been a movie star like the young Clint Eastwood: a strong, lean embodiment of cold masculinity. But it was less his appearance than it was the attitude of this dream character that earned him his nickname.

Mr Wrong embodied all the traits she abhorred in a certain type of man: he was cold, arrogant and sullen, and projected an insufferable air of masculine entitlement. Even physically, though conventionally handsome, he wasn't the type of man she usually found attractive. But if she kept having erotic dreams about Mr Wrong, didn't this mean that she actually wanted a man like him as a lover?

Regarding a dream as a symptom of an underlying complex, or as an expression of a character type, might have led to such a conclusion. But looking at a dream as a kind of text that is amenable to a variety of interpretations allows for a much more flexible response to it. Although the dreamer may be captive to sleep while dreaming, reflecting on it while she is awake enables her to make sense of it in a variety of ways that she may find useful. But there is often a great divergence – a day and night divide of consciousness – between wakefulness and sleep. Olivia may have found Mr Wrong irresistible in her sleep, but awake she found him repellent. So why was there such a gross disparity between her dreaming and waking perceptions of him? Indeed, why did he appear in her dreams as a figure of attraction at all?

If there was a clue to these questions, I suspected it might be found in the fact that Mr Wrong kept appearing in a recurring dream, perhaps as a response to some persistent dissatisfaction in her life. I also wondered if there was a Mr Wrong in her sleep, could she be entertaining an unexpressed hope for an absent Mr Right when she was awake? Her present relationship with Roger barely qualified as a relationship. Although they slept with each other occasionally, neither of them found their lovemaking particularly enjoyable. Nor did they seem to have much to talk about when they spent time together. I wondered how it was possible for Olivia to regard her idle, dispassionate relationship with Roger as romantic at all. Her reply was swift and unequivocal: "Loneliness", she said crisply.

It is tempting to suppose that Mr Wrong appeared in Olivia's dreams in compensation for the unsatisfying relationship she had with Roger. Perhaps this was a factor, though on further reflection, she believed it wasn't so much Roger's shortcomings as a lover as her need to be in a relationship, no matter how unsatisfactory, that made Mr Wrong a symbol of her need to be with a man. What made Mr Wrong so objectionable was that being with him violated her values and sense of who she was. Reflecting further on his image, she realised her need for companionship threatened to override her sense of self-worth, not only in her dreams, but in her love life, as well. The dream brought another, perhaps more valuable insight. She realised that there could never be a Mr Right, an ideal man whose mere appearance would fulfil all her romantic hopes and end her loneliness. Mr Wrong may have appeared in her dreams as the image of a man who gave her respite from her loneliness by virtue of his masculinity alone. But she could never be intimate with someone who was a mere caricature of masculinity and a travesty of her desire. Were these interpretations correct? Only she could decide. But what I considered important was that she remained true to her feelings in considering her dreams, and by this measure her interpretations certainly made sense. For in reflecting on her dreams she was not simply entertaining imaginable, but abstract possibilities; she was also finding the source of her imagination which coloured her sense of self. But how did the exploration of her dreams help her in her waking life?

Olivia did experience modest improvement, though the signs of it weren't particularly dramatic. Her affair with Roger ended quietly by mutual consent, but the vague sense of dissatisfaction that she suffered subsided, as well. Although she had no immediate romantic prospects, she no longer suffered the acute loneliness that had driven her into unsatisfactory relationships, either. More importantly, she decided to be more discriminating in her choice of potential lovers. Better to be alone than be lonely with an unsuitable partner, she realised. A result of her change in attitude was that Mr Wrong ceased to appear in her dreams, indicating the positive change in her. It was more than just dream work that led to her improvement, however. It was, even more, her willingness to engage in the entire therapeutic process that made such a change possible. Dreamwork was only one component of a wider interaction of our work together. Even so, I believe much of our success was due to the trust that we developed through dreamwork.

Trust in psychotherapy is perhaps the most important factor that a therapist can develop in his relationship with a client, but this goes beyond ethical trust, essential though that is. Sensitivity, judgement and intuition are also crucial, but these can only be developed over time through the therapist's attunement to the client's experience. This requires patience and can never be attained once and for all. More often, it is a matter of remaining in sympathetic alignment with the client in her confusion and uncertainty, especially when solutions to her predicament are impossible to find. For trust to hold in these circumstances, a therapist needs to be alert to subtle changes in the client, even when the nature of those changes may not be entirely evident. In any case, it is the attuned awareness of the therapist which conveys his care and encourages her to express herself freely, without fear or inhibition. Exactly how this happens is somewhat mysterious, but working with dreams can strengthen the empathic bond on which therapy depends. I have no shortage of examples, but a few stand out.

A client of mine named Anna, a thoughtful and reflective writer, once described a dream in which she was making her way laboriously through a field of what looked like lavender but was actually marijuana. The plants were tall and abundant which made progress difficult, but she felt she was making headway towards an important destination. As she was recounting the dream, I felt as if I was walking beside her, pushing my way through the thick brush. Then something occurred to me. "There must be a really strong smell here", I commented.

She looked at me with surprise, and confirmed that there was indeed a strong smell, but it wasn't the fragrance of lavender or the pungent aroma of cannabis. It was the foul odour of shit. The rich symbolism of the dream was something we would explore later in depth, but the immediate effect of attunement was to allow me to enter her dream as a living experience and give her the sense that I would be able to follow her wherever her dreams took her. Although this dream did not prove especially significant for the issue that brought her to therapy, it did help to confirm me as a reliable fellow traveller in her inner world and strengthened our therapeutic alliance. I have little doubt that Anna would have done well, even without therapy. What was important for her was that she benefited from it, in part because of what she found through dreamwork. Trust is an essential asset for any therapeutic relationship, even for psychologically robust clients like Anna. But it is even more important in dealing with the dreams of fragile clients. For their nightmares can pose a grave threat to their sense of self, as I found with a client named Ronnie.

Ronnie had been sectioned a number of times long before I met him, but he continued to suffer recurring nightmares originating from the time of his first breakdown. In these terrible dreams, he would be surrounded by several tormentors who taunted him with insults and threats, and he feared he would never be able to make his way home. Afterwards, he would wake up feeling exposed and vulnerable, and become too panic stricken to leave his flat.

Although he knew his fears were caused by his dreams, they were based on actual episodes in his waking life which had occurred years before he came to see me. The bullying happened during a particularly depressing period of his life which eventually led to his hospitalisation. Picking up on his obvious misery, some local youths who gathered on street corners in his neighbourhood used to mock him for their malicious pleasure. Defenceless against their taunts and jibes, Ronnie suffered the added shame of not sticking up for himself. Why he suffered such nightmares years after the actual events that prompted them would always remain an open question. The more pressing matter was to find a way of relieving the intense anxiety his nightmares were causing him. This required a certain sensitivity on my part.

While I wanted Ronnie to be able to find the cause of his nightmares, I also had to be certain that he wouldn't become overwhelmed by them. I knew past traumas can be retriggered without careful safeguarding. I began by asking him if he felt comfortable discussing his nightmares and I let him know that he was free to come out of his recollections whenever he felt he needed to. I also asked him to pause periodically whenever he was recalling a dream so that we were both sure that his connection with me remained secure. At all stages of his recollection, I wanted him to regard me as an ally as he faced the terrors of his dream life. I believed that with support he would be able to go to the source of his dreams and find a safe distance from the terror they caused him. This process took some time, but eventually he was able to find a safe point of entry to explore his dream memories imaginatively. Finding his voice, he spoke to his antagonists directly by telling them to fuck off and leave him alone. This had the effect I had hoped for, as they stopped appearing in his dreams and were exiled to a safe pasture of memory where they no longer threatened him. By finding a voice for his dreams, Ronnie was able to become free of the oppressive memories that haunted him. But he didn't conquer his dreams. He just became less terrified of his dream life.

"It was only a dream", is what caring parents have always murmured to their children after their bad dreams. The importance of such tender concern shouldn't be underestimated, as I know from my own personal experience as a child living in a suburb of Washington DC in 1968, a nightmare of a year in American and world history. One night I woke up screaming from a dreadful dream I was hardly able to remember. Somehow, though, the political assassinations, the race riots and the Vietnam war, all of which convulsed the nation that year, seemed connected to the death of my youngest sister who died a few weeks before my nightmare. It was as if the combined horror of these events had converged on me as I slept, and I suddenly realised how dreadful the world had become. My father came into my bedroom and sat on the edge of my bed, comforting me as I wept. After talking to him, I felt much calmer, even though he didn't dismiss the dream as nonsense. He knew, perhaps even more than I did, the terrible emotional truth of my dream. Dreams exaggerate, distort and defy the laws of reason and logic, yet they can still express the truth of experience by indirect means. Dismissing dreams as irrational or meaningless does nothing to diminish their underlying emotional power. If anything, it makes that underlying power stronger.

"Where id goes, there ego shall be", Freud wrote, stating the aim of psychoanalysis. In his psychology, the id is composed of all the instinctual urges that lie buried beneath the surface of a personality. Although largely unconscious, the id possesses far greater power than the feeble ego with which it is often in conflict. Becoming conscious of these instinctual forces as active influences in the patient's experience requires painstaking work, as Freud knew well from his practice as a psychoanalyst. But by analysing his patients' dreams, he was able to discover the royal road to the unconscious and believed that psychoanalysis offered them a way of travelling it to become free of their psychological suffering. If he erred, it was in believing that the road could be mapped comprehensively, perhaps to a conclusive end. But, as Jung observed, the unconscious really is unconscious, and if the road ends at all, it ends in a place where the light of consciousness never shines. Fortunately, the road of our dreams doesn't simply travel from light to dark; it also travels from darkness to light, pushing towards awareness with an insistent, driving force. And though we may not remember them when we wake up, dreams breach the threshold of consciousness and infuse our first waking moments with the lingering effects of our dreaming. We wake up and find ourselves in the real world again, scarcely aware that our dreams arrived there first, before we did.

Confessions of a Buddhist Psychotherapist

When I first decided to become a psychotherapist, I was determined to have Buddhism feature in my training. I never thought that being a Buddhist would make me a better therapist, nor did I think that therapy should be used to promote the dharma. It was just that Buddhism had helped me personally and made me believe that some of its ideas could be useful for people struggling with their psychological problems. But not all Buddhist therapists are open about their spiritual beliefs, and I know some who firmly believe that whatever religious convictions a therapist might have, those beliefs should never intrude into therapy. Besides, they ask, what makes Buddhist therapists think they're so special? Is it because they're supposed to possess some unique insight into the self and human nature? And are Buddhist clients supposed to get special treatment if they go to see a Buddhist therapist? By wearing our colours so openly, don't we Buddhist therapists run the risk of closing ourselves off from non-Buddhists and retreating, if not into a monastery, then into a safe, cosy environment where only nice, spiritual people would be inclined to go? This sort of criticism usually concludes with something along the following lines: psychotherapy is a treatment for psychological suffering, and a therapy that claims to be Buddhist offers little more than a watered-down version of the Buddhadharma, and may not be true psychotherapy at all. Yet, in spite of all these well-founded objections, I have no reluctance in being open about the importance of Buddhism for my approach to therapy. I will try to explain why here.

Perhaps more than any other profession, psychotherapy depends on the personal history and experience of the practitioner. This doesn't mean that therapists should rely on their personal experience alone, for training and learning from the ongoing experience of seeing clients are essential, too. But few people are likely to become psychotherapists without some affinity for the suffering that therapy deals with, and this often involves having suffered from some psychological affliction themselves. It was certainly the case for me. Years before I became a therapist I suffered from a depression that was severe enough to make me turn to psychotherapy, and even use antidepressants for a time. I vowed then to remember what I was going through so that I could help others who might be experiencing something similar. But suffering from a psychological condition doesn't make someone an expert in it, even though it can increase one's empathy for the suffering of others. In truth, personal experience doesn't become an asset for practising therapy unless it involves a deeper questioning about the self and human nature in general. A theory, or some comprehensive explanation of human experience, is also needed for empathy to link with sound theoretical understanding to become truly effective. For me, Buddhism offers some useful ideas about self-formation and the causes of psychological suffering. But more than anything else, Buddhism gives me faith.

My approach to therapy depends on faith, though not faith in a final salvation, or in some vaunted spiritual goal like enlightenment. It depends on something more fundamental to psychotherapy – the faith that being alive as a human being, even with all the potential for suffering that inheres in the condition, is actually a great blessing. For me, this is no mere piety. It is a way of sustaining hope which I know can be severely tested at times. Every therapist has encountered clients who claimed to feel hopeless. Many of us would also concede that in some cases, our clients' despair seemed justified. The danger for therapists is that the hopelessness of our clients can affect us, too. Loss, trauma, and abuse feature regularly in psychotherapy, and therapists often feel a need to brace ourselves against the pain and confusion that our clients can bring forth. Buddhism is my way of protecting myself against the despair that therapy deals with. But my faith shouldn't be confused for something like the power of positive thinking, or be mistaken for a carte blanche of psychological affirmation. Buddhism begins with a clear-eyed appraisal of existence that seems to offer little hope or consolation to anyone. Existence is suffering, like a sickness without apparent remedy, it claims. Fortunately, the Buddhist analysis doesn't end there.

There is, in fact, an ancient title of the Buddha which refers to him as the Great Physician and builds on the trope by likening the Four Noble Truths, the foundation of Buddhist belief and practice, to a medical procedure consisting of the identification of a disease [*trishna*: suffering], diagnosis [*samadya*: the cause of suffering], prognosis [*nirvana*: the possibility of ending suffering] and a course of treatment [*marga*: the way to end suffering]. Buddhist psychology also provides a useful set of ideas about the underlying causes of psychological suffering, which are known as the three *kleshas*, the defilements which cause suffering: greed [*lobha*], aversion [*dosa*], and delusion [*moha*]. The application of these principles is primarily psychological, and requires the cultivation of qualities that are more psychotherapeutic than medical, more psychic than somatic. The illness he treated, in other words, was largely mental.

When the Buddha began to teach, his instruction was primarily addressed to a monastic audience who were prepared to devote their entire lives to realising his message of spiritual liberation, but he also offered counsel to anybody who asked for it. Though his teaching made some concessions to worldly interests, he taught that the world was a realm to escape, not a place to settle into. Psychotherapy, by contrast, is a manifestly worldly concern which addresses the conflicts and frustrations that arise in the everyday world of love and sex, work and money, conflict and tragedy. If the Buddhist path offers a way of escaping *samsara*, the round of birth and death, psychotherapy establishes its office in the very heart of it. Fortunately, some insights from a Buddhist spiritual practice can still be applied to the problems that psychotherapy deals with, which have everything to do with the client's involvement in the world. But adapting these insights for people in the round of their needs presents a challenge for a Buddhist approach to psychotherapy. This often requires an adaptation of certain key Buddhist concepts for therapeutic use, particularly the paradoxical idea of not-self. Part of my task as a therapist is to make ideas like not-self practicable for my clients in their everyday worlds.

The Psychology of Not-Self

For all its denial of worldly values, Buddhism has always offered a deep analysis of the human condition and a remarkably penetrating description of the mental processes that give rise to the human experience of the world. To Buddhism, it is because of our desires that we come to experience the world at all. There are actually a number of different Buddhist models of mind which have been developed over the course of Buddhist history, but some basic features are common to them all. One of the most fundamental concepts is perhaps more metaphysical than psychological, though it has profound implications for all schools of Buddhist psychology. It consists of a trio of features that characterise all phenomena, known as the Three Marks of Existence---impermanence [*anicca*], suffering [*dukkha*] and not-self [*anatman*]. For Buddhism, these characteristics go together as intrinsic properties of all phenomena, as everything is impermanent, and impermanence is an essential factor of all suffering. Finally, impermanence deprives everything of lasting essence, making everything not self-sufficient, in other words, not-self. This sweeping metaphysical claim not only informs the practice of meditation, it also serves as the foundation for Buddhist psychology.

The central importance of not-self in Buddhist thinking points to an apparent paradox of Buddhist psychology. If the ultimate truth of every phenomenon is that it is not-self, how then do we make sense of being human, of the selves that we experience ourselves to be? And if the ultimate truth of human experience is not-self, then who is supposed to grasp this self-denying principle? In short, how can a way of thought that denies the self be of any use to psychotherapy whose primary concern is, and must be, the self? One point that must be emphasised is that the concept of not-self does not deny a *sense* of self. It is only by appreciating the illusory nature of our sense of self that we can hope to see through it. This is especially important for understanding a Buddhist approach to psychotherapy, for the idea of not-self does not offer a convenient escape from the entanglements of existence, nor does it allow for an abdication of personal responsibility. According to the Buddhist view, taking responsibility for one's thoughts and actions is a prerequisite for realising the liberating potential of the Buddhadharma. Even so, given the central importance of the idea, Buddhist psychotherapy has a unique theoretical problem in reconciling the idea of not-self with the manifest reality of the self that psychotherapy deals with.

My favourite maxim about the Buddhist idea of the self comes from the 13th-century Japanese Zen master, Dōgen, who wrote: "To study the Buddha Way is to study the self. To study the self is to forget the self." By studying the self, Dōgen was referring to *shikantaza*, the method of "just sitting" which characterised his approach to Zen meditation. By forgetting the self, he was referring to dropping the self-preoccupation which influences almost every personal endeavour. Dōgen could have had no inkling that his insight would be relevant to modern psychotherapy, a practice which would have been unimaginable in feudal Japan. Yet, his observation still holds some validity for therapy, especially if we interpret "forgetting the self" as a transformation of personal consciousness freed of compulsive self-concern. In order to appreciate this, however, we need to understand what makes a person's sense of self so important, and how forgetting the self – at least in the sense that Dōgen conceived it – can be useful for therapy.

The Buddhist psychotherapist, Jack Engler, addressed this matter with a memorable one liner: "You have to be somebody before you can become nobody". But his wisecrack makes a serious point. A certain degree of self-possession is required before anyone can attempt to realise the difficult, elusive truth of not-self. But perhaps something else can be added to his observation. No one, not even a Buddha, can realise the ultimate truth of not-self without a considerable impetus from personal experience that drives him to make the realisation. According to Buddhism, it is a person's karma, pushing through innumerable births and deaths, which puts him in an auspicious position for discovering not-self and reaching enlightenment. A similar karmic impetus can move people to undergo therapy, though the reasons for turning to therapy seldom feel auspicious. Moreover, enlightenment, understood as escaping the round of birth and death, is not, and should not, be the goal of therapy. The goal is to help the client make sense of his life and make a meaningful commitment in order to deal with the suffering he experiences. Therapy is, and always must be, a matter of self-concern, particularly within the client's everyday affairs. Yet, from a Buddhist point of view, not-self will always remain the stubborn underlying reality of all experience.

Fortunately for psychotherapy, the idea of not-self can be used like a solvent for freeing the client of his harmful attachments. Letting go of the mistakes, grievances and injustices of the past allows for a freeing disidentification from the pain they cause. By realising that his attachments are inherently not-self, the client can let those harmful attachments go. But letting them go for therapy is not like surrendering to *sunyata,* the great void of emptiness and ultimate reality that underlies everything, as it is for Buddhist meditation. It is more a matter of replacing harmful mental states with more beneficial ones in order to find better self-possibilities. To paraphrase Engler, in order to be somebody, you have to commit to something, that is to say, you have to attach to things that benefit you. But it's important to understand what Buddhism means by attachments.

Self and Attachments

I hardly ever speak about not-self to my clients, as I usually avoid discussing theory in general. And of all theoretical concepts, not-self may be the most open to misinterpretation, and for this reason, I am particularly reluctant to refer to it. By contrast, an interest in attachments has always been important to virtually every school of psychotherapy, as helping clients become more aware of the influence of their attachments is essential for developing self-insight. But this seldom involves a theoretical discussion, as theory may only obscure an insight that should be more emotional than rational, and more embodied than cognitive. But no matter how an insight is made, helping the client realise that his harmful attachments may be the source of his suffering is often the first step towards becoming free of them. So what does Buddhism mean when it refers to attachments?

For Buddhism, attachments are not simply the things and ideas that we decide to adopt as our own. They are, primarily, manifestations of habit patterns that develop from cravings that form in conditions we can't always see. They arise from an unconscious depth with roots that sink deep into craving and aversion. Not all attachments are harmful, and some may even give rise to benign character traits. Moreover, of necessity, everyone will have some attachments, and the way they develop within each of us configures our individual orientations in the world. It is through our attachments – to particular people, things, and ideas, as well as to our social and cultural affiliations – that we experience our lives as meaningful and potentially fulfilling. For this reason, it is impossible not to regard attachments as the substance on which our lives depend. Indeed, we often become most acutely aware of our attachments when we are deprived of them. as their deprivation may cause an excruciating feeling of lack. Such a feeling is one of the most common reasons for people to turn to therapy. But feeling possessed by a harmful attachment– such as an addiction or an obsession, or a self-defeating habit – can produce a similar desperation to be free of it.

My approach in dealing with harmful attachments is to help my clients see that their attachments are contingent on conditions that are changing constantly, and that it is possible to replace harmful attachments with more beneficial ones. I know, however, that giving up attachments is seldom easy for anyone, and that even changing better for worse ones will always require considerable effort. Yet, it is when a person tries to become free of his negative attachments that realising a better potential becomes a real possibility. In Buddhist terms, this could be described as karma, but in therapy it is better regarded as the client becoming more self-aware of the intentional actions that perpetuate his suffering. By developing such an awareness, he can change the direction of his intentional habits and replace blind, harmful attachments with conscious commitments, and find greater freedom for himself. All of this may seem rather abstract, which is a good reason to avoid discussing it in therapy as a theoretical matter. Yet, it should be recognised that following patterns of behaviour thoughtlessly is often the most potent factor in psychological suffering. To become conscious of our deleterious habits is a kind of awakening in itself.

As a therapist, I regularly encounter a number of typical patterns of thought and behaviour in my clients, yet I still wonder why they can't see them. Why, for example, do some people fall repeatedly into unfulfilling or abusive relationships? And why are unwanted, self-destructive habits so difficult for people to break? Above all, why do people perpetuate their own misery with so little understanding of the intentions that cause their suffering? For a Buddhist spiritual practice, waking up to the consequences of our intentional actions represents a crucial first step towards coming to terms with our karma and getting off the treadmill of rebirth. But even in therapy, helping the client become more aware of the hidden motivations for his actions can be deeply liberating. There is just no need to call it karma. There is another, perhaps more compelling, reason to avoid using the idea of karma for therapy. Buddhism advocates a fairly strict code of conduct which follows from a vast and detailed metaphysical vision that is apt to be more haunting than chastening. As a therapist, I have to be far more tolerant and flexible in regarding the mores of my clients. In fact, I must never demand that my clients follow any particular moral code, though I can, and do, try to help my clients find and live by their own moral values. For me, this is seldom a matter of denying my convictions as a Buddhist. Buddhism, after all, is where I find my own moral centre. It not only provides me with spiritual guidance, it also directs me to what I believe is the truth. But how my spiritual convictions influence me in a therapeutic encounter without those beliefs becoming a veiled form of advocacy is one of the things I have to be wary of.

So how can I remain true to Buddhism without imposing my beliefs on my clients? For me, it is a matter of trying to exercise wisdom and compassion.

Wisdom and Compassion

In Buddhism, wisdom complements compassion reaching towards enlightenment like two conjoined wings that enable flight. Therapy, however, must work from the far more modest ambition of improving the everyday prospects of the client and wisely refrains from such a lofty endeavour. Still, in my practice as a therapist, compassion keeps me sensitive to the suffering of my clients, and reminds me of the individual particularity, as well as the sweeping universality, of suffering. And wisdom complements compassion by recognising that each of us comes into the world with a limited perspective that is uniquely our own. Wisdom also reminds me that all human experience emerges from the unfathomable mystery of the self, and tells me that no psychological theory, no matter how far ranging and insightful, can ever reach a comprehensive understanding of any individual's life. In this respect, wisdom depends as much on recognising the limits of my understanding as on applying any knowledge I might possess. Above all, wisdom requires me to remain open to the possibilities of the unknown and the unforeseen.

Whatever wisdom and compassion I hope to bring to my relationship with a client must reach him in terms that will be relevant to his experience. My efforts will always involve learning about his past and the circumstances of his present everyday world. But it will also include becoming acquainted with his inner disposition – his hopes and fears, his affinities and aversions, (often discovered in his dreams and fantasies) – that constitute his sense of self. As our relationship develops and I become more aware of the pattern of his thoughts and feelings, I will be able to appreciate how he experiences himself in his everyday world. I will learn much of this through our verbal interactions, but a great deal will also be gathered simply by being in his presence. I refer to this heightened sense of being in a client's presence as attunement, and If I am properly attuned, I will reach an understanding of what it is like to be in his skin. I would even say I will be able to peer into his soul, were it not for the fact that the idea of the soul earns disapproval from both Buddhism and psychotherapy.

There are good reasons for psychotherapy to look askance at any ideas that come from religion, which is why therapy has always preferred to present itself as an heir of medical science. Most therapists would also recognise that there is a danger in flirting with any notion that therapy might possess a spiritual authority or be able to dispense absolution for psychological complaints. Yet, insofar as it refers to the unique, largely hidden, inner character of each individual, the idea of a soul retains a certain indispensable value for me as a therapist. Still I must avoid using the term, much as I avoid using terms like karma and not-self. Yet, there are times when, for all my training and experience as a therapist, I feel clueless before the inherent mystery of a client's life. Sometimes, I simply don't know why a client is as he is. No less important, I know that he may be more bewildered about himself and his condition than I am. I also know that he may find within himself hidden resources and latent possibilities that neither of us may be able to see, but which can be discovered through our interactions. This is not a religious idea that leads to eternal salvation. It is an approach to therapy that insists on recognising the inherent mystery of every person's life.

The Soul of Buddhist Therapy

The idea of a soul invokes a related idea about a person's deepest urge to find fulfilment, and even transcendence, through the mystery of his being. This is usually understood as a mystical undertaking but, in therapy, mystical longings are generally and wisely regarded with deep suspicion. For the point of therapy is not to escape to a transcendent realm; it is to find meaning and authentic possibility in the client's everyday world.

Therapy often begins to find traction when the client makes an introspective turn and discovers that everything he seeks arises from his longings and appetites. His urges, confused and conflicted as they often are, still drive him to search for some elusive, unknown thing that will bring lasting satisfaction to his life. In truth, he is engaged in an endless quest to secure a sense of self. Such a manifestly existential quest may seem to have little to do with the more immediate problems that typically bring people to therapy, but it is actually the root of a mystery that gives rise to virtually everyone's sense of self. According to Buddhism, it is this relentless, unconscious search for a secure, lasting self which is the true source of the *ahamkara*, the I-maker, that perpetuates our conflicted sense of self in the world. Buddhism goes on to assert that it is only by dropping our compulsive self-preoccupation that we will ever be able to see the actual truth of our being, freeing us to experience life without a compulsive need for self-validation. For most of us, though, this ideal may seem too self-denying, even ascetic for our everyday affairs, and it seldom, if ever, accords with the interests of therapy. For our identities remain dependent on being recognised for who we are, and finding a place in the world as we experience it. For this reason, unlike a Buddhist spiritual practice which aims to surpass self-interest altogether, therapy must strive to deepen the self-awareness of the client in his self-bound attempts to find satisfaction in his everyday world. Yet, even here, Buddhism offers an insight regarding impermanence that can be useful for psychotherapy – but only if therapy is allowed to address an intractable problem that everyone must confront.

It is easy to ignore the fact that both the source and destination of personal experience – birth and death – mark the beginning and end points between which we must deal with our everyday affairs to become ourselves. "Where did I come from before I was born?" and "What will happen to me when I die?" can seem pointless, evasive questions, especially when there are more immediate concerns to face. Yet, anyone who attempts a thorough self-reckoning must address these questions, even though they mostly hover in the background of everyday life. That we are all born and will all die are flat truths from one perspective. But from another, they are indicators of an unfathomable mystery that we are forced to live out, but are unable to solve. It is a mystery we are forced to confront whenever we encounter the reality of death. As a therapist, I often see people who have lost, or are about to lose, someone close to them. Sometimes, a client may even be facing the prospect of imminent death himself. It almost always comes as a shock, despite the fact that everyone claims to believe in their own mortality. But once the shock passes, a question arises naturally, even if it often goes unspoken: given the fact that you are going to die, what are you going to do now to make your life meaningful for you? During a death watch, the question becomes virtually irrepressible. But Buddhism asserts that this question is always with us, whether we are aware of it or not.

It may be possible for the paths of Buddhism and psychotherapy to converge, at least for a few clients. But, as a therapist, it is not my place to suggest a spiritual path; it is my task to help my clients find whatever path is right for them. As a Buddhist, though, I sometimes wonder if my work is in keeping with the moral precepts of Buddhism. When, for example, I encourage my clients to find a path based on their own freely chosen values, am I actually helping them better their lives, or am I condoning a way of life that Buddhism might regard as *akusala,* or unskillful? The answer isn't always clear. But I hold to the belief that what Buddhism calls *avidya,* or ignorance, is at the root of all intentional actions that cause suffering. My hope is to help them dispel their ignorance so they can truly see what causes their suffering. This may, or may not, lead them to find a spiritual path for themselves. But as a therapist, that is not and cannot be my concern.

My belief in Buddhism doesn't provide me with any privileged knowledge for psychotherapy, any more than my practice of therapy makes me a better Buddhist. But therapy does give me a vantage point for observing the experience of my clients in their everyday worlds, while Buddhism sharpens my sense of wonder at being existent at all. In this connection, I always think of the Buddha's own moment of seminal wonder as a boy sitting under a rose apple tree, watching his father's fields being ploughed on a beautiful spring day. What of all the worms and insects that were dislodged and eaten by birds as their habitats were being destroyed? Were their painful deaths all that could be expected for all mortal creatures? he wondered. There could be no simple factual answers to his question. Facts would only allow the flat observation that this is how the world is. Yet, at this precise moment when he might have turned away from an unanswerable mystery, the boy fell spontaneously into meditative rapture and kept alive the spark of wonder that could only have been extinguished by strict objective reasoning. Later, the memory of this episode inspired him to meditate in his own way which gave rise to the deep insights that made him a Buddha. I am no Buddha, but as a therapist I try to be like that boy under the rose apple tree. In a world I can't imagine being more beautiful, I am awed by the seemingly infinite variety of suffering that I witness here.

Yet my faith in therapy – a faith which depends on my faith in Buddhism – gives me hope. By trying to understand my clients, I try to help them understand themselves. I begin with an unspoken request: "Tell me who you are." The answer seldom, if ever, turns out to be what I thought it would be.

Closure

Kate comes into the consulting room with quiet ease and a relaxed expression on her face. Everything in the room is familiar to her now, and as she takes her seat it is as if the chair belongs to her. Perhaps in a way it does, at least for this hour. For she has been keeping her weekly appointment more or less regularly for over a year and a half, and during her appointed time she knows the office will be as much hers as mine. Though our greeting is friendly and rather informal, I still observe her closely for an indication of any change in her mood since I last saw her. But I detect no signs of anxiety or consternation and note only that she is dressed in lighter clothing now that the weather has turned warmer. She asks about me, and I reply I am fine, but with a smile that indicates that though I appreciate her courtesy, I will have nothing further to say about myself. She seems to understand my unstated intention and smiles in return. We both know that nothing would be gained by talking about me, and our focus will be on her, just as it always has been. Still, I find it reassuring that she enquires about me with such casual friendliness, which leads me to expect that this will be an agreeable appointment. We are ready to begin.

Although we are relaxed about her personal situation now, this has not always been the case. Much has changed since we first met, not only in the familiarity we feel with each other, but also in Kate's circumstances. Her relationship, which had first prompted her to seek therapy, ended a couple of months after she began to see me. The breakup followed her discovery that her partner had been cheating on her throughout their relationship. She felt devastated at the time, but her bitter disappointment was followed by a long period of reflection which led to an important change in her. She realised that all her attempts to find a partner had always been conditioned by an unexpressed belief that she would never find anyone who would be able to accept her as she really was. She even thinks that she chose her previous partner because she had a hunch he would be unfaithful. Now she realises she has to be more careful in choosing a partner if she hopes to find someone who is truly interested in her. Although Kate has not entered into another relationship since her break-up, she has done some casual dating in recent months, and feels both desirable and open to desire, important indicators that she feels alive in her skin again. More importantly, she no longer complains about depression or anxiety, and feels no need for medication. And for more than a month now, we have been wondering if she is ready to terminate.

Termination is a rather formal way of ending a therapeutic relationship, but it is not necessarily how all therapeutic relationships end. Sometimes, clients simply quit without any notification at all. But when a relationship has gone on long enough and has reached a sufficient level of trust, terminating formally feels natural, like a long journey reaching its intended destination. Ideally, things will get wrapped up neatly in a last session, but in practice this rarely happens. Of course, the issues that she first brought into therapy should have been adequately addressed, but often those issues will present themselves in other ways. This is certainly the case with Kate. The problem in her relationship turned out to be the infidelity of her partner, but now that she is free of him she still questions her capacity for trust. She wonders, for example, if she is at risk of finding herself with someone who may be no more trustworthy than her previous partner. She would also like to know what I think.

I tell her that people often choose a partner who replicates the character traits of someone who first attracted their interest. The pattern is often established by the child's relationship to a parent. If the parental relationship was loving and supportive, the child will be more likely to choose someone who will meet her emotional needs as an adult. Kate says nothing in response to this, but given her difficult history with her father, perhaps she thinks that her prospects of finding a loving, trustworthy partner aren't very promising. But then, dropping the tone of the wise, all-knowing therapist, I tell her that I don't know what will happen.

Though I consider it virtually inarguable that everyone will be deeply influenced by their relationships with their primary caregivers, I don't believe it's the only thing that determines a person's course in life. Moreover, Kate has pursued therapy with admirable dedication to change, and I have few reservations about her essential honesty and willingness to act in good faith. I have meagre talents as a prophet, but I still like her chances of finding someone she can trust and love. Still, there is no way of knowing what will happen. Only time will tell, probably when she is long out of therapy.

I've had clients in the past whose departure from therapy felt doubtful to me, usually because the concerns that first made them seek help didn't seem adequately resolved. Some clients simply say they've had enough, implying that they no longer felt I could help them. Others declare they're feeling much better and that therapy has helped them achieve their goals. But unless I detect an underlying change of heart, I tend to be sceptical of such claims. It is rare, however, for me to express my scepticism openly. I simply let them know my door will be open to them if they feel a need to return. Occasionally clients do come back, but more often I never hear from them again. Sometimes I wonder if another therapist might suit them better. But I don't think psychotherapy is for everyone, or that it's the only way for people to make meaningful changes in their lives. But for Kate, therapy appears to have given her what she needed.

But what did Kate need? A better approach to relationships and deeper self-insight are what she first wanted out of therapy, and there certainly have been significant improvements in both areas. But therapy is not simply a way of solving problems, even though personal problems are the stuff of therapy. At a deeper level, it's a way of helping clients make sense of their lives beyond putting immediate frustrations to rest. I think of this as a kind of centring, though I seldom use this expression in speaking to clients. Yet, when a client finds her centre, she will be able to find the resolution she needs to deal with whatever problems are likely to arise in her life. This offers no simple path to happiness, but it will put her in a better position to discover what she really wants and who she truly is. But then, how is it possible for anyone to be entirely sure of who she is? Only by living and trying to remain as true to her beliefs and values as she can. It is what I mean by finding her centre. But finding one's centre isn't accomplished once and for all. It's a lifelong discovery, a way of orienting oneself in the face of constantly changing conditions. A kind of mystery, in other words.

By now Kate is comfortable with the idea of not knowing what she is likely to experience in the future, for not knowing has been a leitmotif of our work together. She also realises that not knowing does not mean surrendering to ignorance, but means cultivating an attitude of meaningful wonder. This involves a certain amount of conscious reflection on her part, but it's also about remaining open to unforeseen possibilities emerging in unexpected ways. Not knowing is the condition in which each of us has to begin our search for personal truth. But not everyone believes they need to find their truth. Fewer still would imagine that they can only find it by first realising how little they know about themselves. But it's a realisation – often a painful one – that moves many people to turn to therapy.

A silence has now settled over us, which is not quite the same as other silences we have experienced before. At first, our silences could be quite tense, but over time they have become more thoughtful and reflective, sometimes even peaceful. But there is uncertainty about where we are at this moment. Still, though we both wonder what's on each other's minds, we aren't apprehensive about what might – or might not – emerge if one of us chooses to speak. Even so, the natural rhythm and flow of our verbal exchange seems to have come to a temporary halt. Finally, I decide to say something and ask Kate if she has anything else on her mind.

"Not really", she says. "I'm actually feeling quite content."

"That sounds good. But do you think your contentment will last?"

"Of course not", she replies, smiling. "Don't you always say nothing lasts forever?"

"Sometimes I do", I admit. "But do you think you'll be able to handle adversity if things aren't going so well?"

"I think so", she says, before adding more emphatically, "Yes, I actually do. I think I'm handling things better already."

"Yes", I say, nodding. "I think so, too."

She pauses for a moment before she says: "I don't feel particularly optimistic. But I don't have the feeling that the sky is about to fall on me anymore, either."

"That sounds pretty good. But would you like anything to happen?"

"A relationship would be nice – a good one, that is."

"It seems you're working on that."

"Yes, but not desperately. I want one, but not desperately."

"I agree, But what happens if you don't find anyone you like?"

"I don't know. The important thing is not to accept someone I know won't be right for me. I just need to be careful – and patient."

I nod in agreement again, though in fact I'm more apprehensive about this answer than about anything Kate has said before. It's not her answer itself that concerns me. It's the rather brutal market for relationships she faces, which places a premium on quick transactions of desire and discounts the rewards of intimacy and trust. But she knows this marketplace well – better, in fact, than I do – and is as well equipped to handle it as anyone. I still hope she finds someone suitable. But the matter is not in my hands.

"So you think I'm going to be alright?" she asks ingenuously.

"Alright to do what?"

"To not need therapy any more."

"I think I trust your judgement on this matter. But what do you think?"

"I have got a lot out of it. I think I'll probably miss it, too. But I think it's enough for now."

I say nothing in reply, but simply nod in agreement.

"Are we finished, then?"

"It's up to you. But I certainly think you'll be okay if you decide to leave."

"And if I need to, will I be able to come back?"

"Sure, you can always come back. But you may not feel any need to."

"I hope I won't. But it's nice to know that I always can. I appreciate it."
And I nod to acknowledge her thanks.

There is a brief awkward moment now as our work together seems to be done, but there are still a few more minutes left in our appointment. I don't want to hasten her departure, but like Kate I can't think of anything more to say. Finally, she breaks the silence.

"So, is this it ?" she asks.

"It seems like it to me."

"Then should I leave now?"

"You don't have to. We still have a few minutes left. But if you'd like to go, you're certainly free to do so."

She shrugs and smiles with mock embarrassment, before she gets up out of her chair. I rise out of mine and watch her as she picks up her handbag and prepares to leave. She looks over to me, and then with a facial expression that seems filled with mixed emotions, she steps over and hugs me. It is the first and only time we have had physical contact other than a handshake. It is certain to be the last, as well. I walk with her to the door of the consulting room, and as she steps into the hallway she turns around and gives me a little wave.

"Take care", I say.

After Kate leaves I scribble a few notes before my next client arrives, noting the positive way we closed today. I am pleased that we were able to work so well together and that she was satisfied by what therapy gave her. In the past, I used to fret over all the mistakes I thought I might have made with clients – the things I failed to notice, or the remarks I should have made. Now, I just try to learn from whatever errors I make. I know I will never be perfect. Some things will always escape my understanding. I will never be as perceptive as I would like to be. But I hope to keep learning as I go along, and if I work long enough with a client, I will always discover something new as a therapist. As for my clients, it is what they discover about themselves and can use to improve their lives that makes therapy worthwhile. Uncovering the mystery of their everyday lives may not be the way they think about therapy, but helping them find new perspectives to improve their prospects is what I believe psychotherapy is all about.

It takes time, patience and much uncertainty, with no guaranteed outcomes beyond what our shared commitment to being truthful can offer. But I can't dwell much longer on these ideas now. Another client will be arriving shortly, and I need to review my notes before he arrives. I wonder how he will be doing today.

Thanks to...

A number of people provided me with help and advice, which made this book possible. The first person to thank is Caroline Brazier, who has given me so much support over the years that I can hardly begin to account for it all.

Suffice it to say that I would not be the psychotherapist that I am now without her generous help and thoughtful guidance. I would also like to thank Andrew Carey, the publisher of Triarchy Press, whose patience, wisdom and expert editing has made this book possible. I am also grateful to Bo Gort, a friend and fellow trainee at Tariki Psychotherapy Programme, who designed the cover of this book beautifully, using the painting 'Two Blind Men Crossing a Log Bridge' by Hakuin Ekaku for the central image. Most of all, I owe a huge debt of gratitude to all my clients, none of whom can be named, but whose influence on me in writing this book cannot be overestimated.

Books Mentioned in the Text

A Path With a Heart [Rider, 2002] Jack Kornfield is a psychotherapist who spent years as a monk in the Thai Forest Tradition, training under the renowned meditation master, Ajahn Chah. Kornfield recognised that he and other Western monks often used mediation to avoid the psychological problems they suffered.

Collected Poems [Farrar, Strauss, & Giroux, 1989] Aubade was Larkin's last published poem. Appropriately, it offers a disquieting meditation on mortality and impending death.

The Dhammapada [Penguin Classics, 2010] Valerie Roe's translation of the classic Buddhist text.

Dreams [Routledge Classics. 2002] Jung broke from Freud, his erstwhile mentor, by arguing that dreams did more than disguise conflicts that would otherwise disturb a dreamer's sleep. His research into dreams reflected his original understanding of unconscious processes.

Love's Executioner [Penguin, 2013] Irving Yalom, an existential psychiatrist and psychotherapist, presents a highly readable collection of clinical tales.

In Dreams Begin Responsibilities and Other Stories [Souvenir Press, 2003] Delmore Schwartz, an American literary figure of the post-war period, was influenced in his most famous short story by psychoanalysis. The title comes from the poem 'Responsibilities' by W. B. Yeats.

Interpretation of Dreams {Oxford University Press, 2008] Sigmund Freud's classic study of dreams which was foundational for psychoanalysis and has influenced the modern approach to dream interpretation since it was first published.

The Politics of Experience [Penguin Books, 1967] R.D. Laing, a radical psychiatrist who became famous in the 1960s, argued that family dysfunction is the principal factor in causing serious mental illness. His freewheeling approach to psychotherapy emphasised the personal dynamic between therapist and client.

Taking Care: An Alternative to Therapy [Constable, 1998] David Smail, a clinical psychologist, argues that the human craving for love and security disposes people to surrender their independence in order achieve what are in fact unattainable goals. Modern consumerism exploits this insecurity for its own gain. Therapy sometimes aggravates the problem by supporting the illusions consumerism promotes.

Transformations of Consciousness [New Science Library, 1986] Jack Engler, a psychotherapist with extensive experience as a student and teacher of meditation, studied in India under Dipa Ma, a renowned master of vipassana. A cofounder of the Insight Meditation Centre in Barre, Massachusetts, he acts as a supervisor for psychotherapy at Harvard Medical School.

About the Author

R. J. Chisholm is a psychotherapist and counsellor who practises in Canterbury, UK. He co-edited, and contributed to *The Wisdom of Not-Knowing*, published by Triarchy Press. A practitioner of meditation for more than thirty years, he draws on Buddhist psychology in his practice as a therapist.

Also from Triarchy Press

The Wisdom of Not-Knowing: Essays on psychotherapy, Buddhism and life experience – Bob Chisholm and Jeff Harrison
In daily life, when we see, hear or touch something that we don't recognise, we are instantly at our most alert. In that condition of 'not-knowing' we are in a state of alive, lithe awareness: asking questions, inviting input, open to learning, looking for significance and meaning…

These essays, most by practising psychotherapists, some of them Buddhists, take as their starting point the idea that not-knowing is fundamental to conscious reflection and the desire to know must always arise in the first instance from the self-awareness of not-knowing.

Nothing Special: Experiencing Fear and Vulnerability in Daily Life
– Mary Booker
A collection of poetry, prose, photographs and personal experience, written by a noted dramatherapist on the experience of vulnerability. Mary explores the roots of vulnerability and fear in her own life, then uses four characters from Shakespeare's *Tempest* to unpick the different faces of fear that arise when we meet rejection, abandonment, oppression, alienation, objectification, chaos and a sense of being out-of-control.

Being with Others: Curses, spells and scintillations
– Nelisha Wickremasinghe
Being human is not easy. The capabilities and qualities we have acquired in our long evolution are both a blessing and a curse. Our ability to think and remember, and our propensity to care for each other and make sophisticated civilisations, can work against us. When they do, they show up in our lives as curses. This book explores how five curses are cast into and influence our lives and uncovers the spells we hope will break them. It shows that our most trusted spell – the belief that a special Other can heal, protect and save us – does not (and will not) work. Which invites the question: what will free us from our curses?

Beyond Threat: Finding your centre in the midst of uncertainty and change – Nelisha Wickremasinghe

Unless we are in physical danger few of us think we are living 'under threat'. Yet our brains believe we are at risk many times a day. Nowhere is this more true than at work, where our response to deadlines, cuts, abrasive managers, competitive colleagues and dissatisfied customers is too often controlled by a part of our brain that's better suited to detecting, devouring or running away from predators. This is our threat brain, and on its own it is little help in dealing with the complex challenges of organisational life.

Psychologist and leadership consultant Dr. Nelisha Wickremasinghe takes us beyond the threat brain and describes the workings of our Trimotive Brain which can respond with intelligence and compassion to unwanted and unpleasant life experiences – if we learn how to manage it.

Encounters with the "Other": A History and Possibilities
– Barry Oshry

This book ends with a 'catalogue of catastrophes' reaching from the ethnic cleansing of the Rohingya of Myanmar, back through the Holocaust to the Armenian genocide – a reminder, if any were needed, that contemporary societies have not lost their taste for identifying and labelling the 'others' in their midst and slaughtering them. Indeed populist governments positively rely on the cohesion that can be found in bringing a group of people together in the face of an external threat. Barry Oshry uses the lenses of 'loose and tight', 'liberal and conservative', 'pure and conflicted', 'tolerance and purity' to highlight the range of reflexive responses we can have to 'others in our midst' especially when we are under the stress of poverty, lack of housing or shortage of jobs. He shows how these responses can be characterised as seeing through Power or Love. Finally he suggests how the intolerant 'Power cycle' can be interrupted and tempered by the more inclusive 'Love cycle' to prevent further catastrophes.

www.triarchypress.net

Lightning Source UK Ltd.
Milton Keynes UK
UKHW030810090222
398417UK00006B/180